BOXING IN LEEDS AND BRADFORD

BOXING
IN LEEDS & BRADFORD

by
Ronnie Wharton

Wharncliffe Books

First Published in 2001 by
Wharncliffe Books
an imprint of
Pen and Sword Books Limited,
47 Church Street, Barnsley,
South Yorkshire. S70 2AS

For up-to-date information on other titles produced under the
Wharncliffe imprint, please telephone or write to:

> **Wharncliffe Books**
> **FREEPOST**
> **47 Church Street**
> **Barnsley**
> **South Yorkshire S70 2BR**
> **Telephone (24 hours): 01226 - 734555**

ISBN: 1-903425-10-7

A CIP catalogue record of this book is available from the
British Library

Cover illustration: Richard Dunn and Muhammad Ali in Munich,
Germany, 1976. *Telegraph & Argus*

Printed in Great Britain by
CPI UK

CONTENTS

ABOUT THE AUTHOR

Born in Bradford in 1944, Ronnie Wharton's first interest in boxing came from the early fifties radio boxing nights and the broadcasts of commentator Eamonn Andrews and his summariser Barrington Dalby. A collector of scrap books and memorabilia since those days led to him writing a successful series of newspaper articles on the history of the sport published in the late seventies and early eighties.

A revival in the sport in recent years with both Bradford and Leeds boasting British champions had led him to compile the definitive history of the game in the two sport rivalling cities. Ronnie's first involvement with Wharncliffe Books came two years ago when he was one of the authors in *Aspects of Bradford*. Last year Wharncliffe published *Boxing in South Yorkshire* and Ronnie is currently working on a third book featuring Yorkshire boxing heroes, which will feature fighters from all corners of the county. Any enthusiasts who want to submit boxers' names for consideration can write to Ronnie Wharton, c/o Wharncliffe Books.

Dedication

I would like to dedicate this book to the memory of two great stalwarts of Bradford boxing - Jim Emmett, a promoter at the Olympia in the 1930s and manager of several fighters including Mick Melia and Jimmy Mahoney, son of Paddy, Bradford's first glove champion and a top referee throughout the thirties into the fifties, who gave me hours of time and who could both verify and enlarge upon any fresh information I had come across. There was many a fruitful Sunday morning at Jim's house at Eccleshill and Friday nights in Low Moor over a pint at the Harold Club with Jimmy Mahoney. The late Jim Windsor was extremely helpful on the Leeds scene and I am indebted to Harold Beckett who was Hal Bairstow's manager who was a feast of knowledge on boxing in Keighley.

Once again I am grateful to Bill Matthews for photographs and Ann Marie-Leach for putting the work on to disc.

Acknowledgements

The Author thanks the following for the use of illustrations within his book: The Bradford *Telegraph & Argus*, Tommy Madden, Boxing 1913, the Blackbrough family, Leeds Old Boxers, the Rowan family, the late Jimmy Mahoney, the late Jim Emmett, Croydon Old Boxers, Jack Marchant, Percy Vear, Arthur Barnes, Bill Sedgwick, Harold Beckett, Jim Windon, the Delaney family, David Jackman, Frank Grant and Bill Matthews.

CHAPTER 1

'Brassey'
and the Prize Fight Era

From a sport which first became popular in the early years of the eighteenth century, James Figg is acknowledged as the first British champion. A title which he won in 1719, a year which is accepted as the starting date for what has become the most popular sport in the world.

During this early history of the bare-fist prize fight era, the only Yorkshireman with legitimate claims as a contender for championship honours was John Leechman, who was better known in the pugilistic arena as 'Brassey'. Leechman, whose height was 6ft and weighed 12 stone 4lb was born in Bradford on 1 January 1815. His first recorded battle was in 1831, when at the age of sixteen he defeated Thomas Hartley at Eccles Moor near Leeds, after a tough fight lasting an hour and a quarter. In August of the same year, he took

'Brassey'. 12,000 people saw him fight on Baildon Moor.

the same time to batter Ned Batterson in a fight for £5 a side although one report gives the result to Batterson. During 1833 'Brassey' had two successful fights in Lancashire. In the first, against George Ireson at Salford, he won in twenty minutes, while the second, at Harpen Hag near Manchester against Young Winterflood of Nottingham, ended in dispute, although 'Brassey' claimed the decision.

'Brassey's fame spread locally and there was a 12,000 crowd to see his next battle at Baildon Moor in 1835 against Leeds based Irishman, Jem Bailey. Despite rumours that 'Brassey' was badly out of condition, he won a fight for £10 a side and lasting 135 minutes

Benjamin Caunt, 6ft 2in English champion in the bare knuckle era.

William Thompson, known as 'Bendigo', one of the immortals of the prize ring.

covering seventy-four rounds. Rounds were not as they are today. When a man went down it signalled the end of the round, so some rounds lasted only seconds. Early in 1836 'Brassey' disposed of Tom Scruton who claimed to be the Yorkshire champion. Needing only twenty minutes he proved the winner in a fight for £20 a side. 'Brassey' adopted the loser's title.

At the same time as 'Brasseys' reputation was growing in the North, in the Midlands, a certain William Thompson who boxed under the soubriquet of 'Bendigo' and later to be famed as one of the immortals of the prize ring, was making similar strides in the rich vein of fistic talent around Nottingham. 'Bendigo's reputation had been built on his defeat of fellow Nottingham pugilist Ben Caunt, later to follow 'Bendigo' as English champion. 'Bendigo', much the lighter man at under 12 stone, had been the equal of the giant 6ft 2in, 14¹/₂ stone Caunt and immediately there was talk of a match between him and the champion, Deaf Burke.

In November 1835, 'Brassey' announced by letter in Bell's Life that he was prepared to meet 'Bendigo' halfway between Nottingham and Bradford for £50 aside. For a while the challenge was side stepped as 'Bendigo' toured the country giving exhibitions of his strength and agility. But when 'Brassey' renewed his challenge, saying that he was open to fight any twelve stone man within 100 miles of Bradford for £25 or £50 and saying that his money was at the *Stags Head,* Sheffield, the match came into being. It was made for £25 a side and held nine miles from Sheffield on the Doncaster road on an open space known as Stocks Moor. The fight lasted seventy minutes over fifty-two rounds. 'Bendigo's 'superiority in science' according to one report, was the main factor in a most severe fight which ended with 'Bendigo' winning after the Bradford man had committed a

'Brassey', Bradford's prize fight champion. *Telegraph & Argus*

foul blow. 'Brassey' and his backers not satisfied with the defeat immediately proposed a fresh match for £50, but 'Bendy' elected to seek fresh pastures in London.

Jem Bailey, beaten by 'Brassey' in their first fight demanded a return clash. Before this he had sought a fight with 'Bendigo' which had fallen through after terms had been agreed when the Irishman's backers had pulled out. The second battle was at Hales Green, Norfolk and although 'Brassey' won in the seventy-first round, Bailey's backers raised a dispute over a piece of indecision by the referee and sued the stakeholders and successfully recovered their money.

Meanwhile 'Bendigo' and Ben Caunt had fought their second great battle and Caunt had won after 'Bendigo' collapsed and was disqualified for going down without being struck. In February 1839 'Bendigo' beat the English champion, Deaf Burke, who had returned from an American tour, and the Nottingham hero was acclaimed champion. Despairing of ever having a second crack at 'Bendigo', 'Brassey' took a fight against the other leading Northern contender, Young Langan of Liverpool. It was fought at Woodhead in Cheshire and the Yorkshireman was specially trained by a name from the pugilistic past, Ned Painter. After seventy-five rounds lasting two hours and thirty-five minutes, 'Brassey' was acclaimed winner when Langan with both eyes closed, was unable to come out at the bell.

'Brassey's championship hopes took another back seat when magistrates in Salford, in an effort to suppress pugilism, indicted him for causing a riot after an incident in a fight which he had seconded in Manchester. He was sentenced to two months' imprisonment.

In March 1840 'Bendigo' badly twisted a knee. For a while he was unable to walk and he announced his retirement from the ring. Deaf Burke immediately reclaimed the title, but in his first defence in September 1840, he was badly beaten by Mick Ward.

With 'Bendigo' out of the way, 'Brassey' turned his attention to 'Bendigo's main rival , Ben Caunt. The match was fixed at £100 a side fought at Six Miles Bottom, near Cambridge. The Bradford man went as far as to send Caunt a poem:-

> *To thee I send these lines, illustrious Caunt*
> *Of courage tried, and huge as John of Gaunt*
> *To thee my foolscap with ink I blot*
> *To tell the big 'un Brassey fears him not*
> *Prove that in fight one Briton can surpass thee*
> *And if you seek his name, I thunder Brassey*

Caunt was much the bigger man and 'Brassey' was conceding 2¹/₂ stone. To avoid trouble with the establishment, the fight started at 9am, but torrential rain made the field waterlogged. The excess weight was too much for 'Brassey' and Caunt finished much the stronger. In a ninety-minute fight, there were over a hundred rounds and 'Brassey' went down in most of them. Despite protests from the backers, the Bradford man would not quit and he finished the fight collapsed in total exhaustion. His valiant display was honoured by a collection from the patrons, which realised £40. Caunt went on to beat Ward the following year to win the championship outright.

After a period of inactivity, 'Brassey' accepted a challenge from Tass Parker of West Bromwich. Difficulty in finding a mutually agreed venue arose when authorities in Nottinghamshire and Derbyshire moved the participants out of their counties. After many difficulties, a field was found in which it was said a small bank divided the two counties of York and Derby. Even this was found unsuitable and the two fighters set off on their horses and carts to find an alternative arena. Eventually, after they had been on the move all day, the fight took place at Brunt Leys near Worksop. The result was that 'Brassey' was beaten in another marathon lasting 170 minutes and needing 158 rounds. 'Brassey' the 6-4 favourite took another beating, his reputation as a non-quitter carrying him through many rounds when he seemed oblivious as to what was going on. 'Brassey's backer, 'King Dick', seeing his fighter's folly refused to second for him and after a while 'Brassey' listened to the demands of his friends and quit.

This was 'Brassey's last fight. During February 1844, 'Bendigo' who had returned to the ring and was challenging champion Caunt for a third meting sent 'Brassey' a valentine: -

Many happy returns of the spring, bouncing Brassey
I hope fortune gives you no cause to complain
That you're right as a trivet, determined and saucy
And ready for mischief with Bendy again.

Brassey was unable to find backers for the match, for the gallant fighter was on a downhill course and he died in 1845, mainly as a result of his epic battles in the ring. He was only thirty. At the time of his death, his two great rivals, Caunt and 'Bendigo' met for a third time and 'Bendigo' retained the championship.

Prize Fighting in Leeds
The first Leeds prizefighter to reach prominence was Bill Riley, who had at least four fights in the 1830s. He had a quick victory over McGregor in a £10 match in Leeds in 1834 and beat Sam Pixton in a fight at Norland Moor, lasting fifty-three minutes later in the year. By 1839 he was fighting for £50 and beat Robert Holmes at Rawdon, although there was a wrangle over the stakes. He met his match in Dick Holmes of Birstall in another £50 fight, the latter winning in twenty rounds.

Holmes fought a memorable bout the same year with George Sinclair ('The Young Slasher') lasting 140 minutes at Salters Brook, the decision being a draw. He had two clashes with Bill Hackney of Hull, which both ended in unsatisfactory results. The first at Hadfield lasted twenty-six minutes and although Holmes was given the verdict, it was decided that Holmes should forfeit £20 to Hackney and a rematch to take place. The second fight at Tadcaster, had a similar conclusion. It was alleged that Holmes had hit foul and there was another wrangle over the stakes.

To reduce the chances of arrest pseudonyms were used. An example was a match at Quarry Hill in 1841, between the 'Pocklington Youth' and the 'Lancashire Jew', which was won by the Yorkshire lad. Fights reported in the press would refer to the participants in similar style. Thus we had a 'Winking Tom' who was beaten by George Child in Leeds in 1840 and an earlier 'Young Brad' who drew with 'Jones the Welsh' near Dewsbury, the fight being stopped by the police.

'A disgusting exhibition of disgraceful and brutalising scenes' was how the *Bradford Observer* reported a fight on Rombalds Moor in

1850. The opponents bruised and battered each other before the 15,000 crowd. The action ended after seventeen minutes when Seargent of Huddersfield, the only man on his feet, claimed a £50 side bet. A further fight scheduled at Baildon Moor in 1863 was prevented from taking place by a strong body of constables who dispersed a large, expectant crowd who had gathered first thing in the morning. Police action again prevented a fight five years later at Stay Hill off Rooley Lane. One of the culprits, Mark Coleman, was pointed out to Sergeant Laycock of Bowling and he immediately gave chase. Coleman collapsed after a four-mile chase and the next day he was fined £10 and ordered to keep the peace for three months.

Though the authorities expressed wishes that the working class would find better ways of demonstrating their manliness, the sport flourished underground and as many as 30,000 attended a fight at Bradford Moor.

Two of Leeds most celebrated fighters were the diminutive 8 stone, William Mills and Tommy Smith, who weighed in at 9st 9lbs. Mills' first recorded fight was a victory over William Bowers at Leeds in 1840. He went onto a win over another Leeds fighter, Clarke at Fryston, as well as beating Joe Brook in seventy-three minutes at Pontefract. He was then matched against Enoch Horridge at Manchester for £25. Horridge had served a sentence for his involvement in the sport and was later to serve another. Horridge got the verdict but it took him 165 minutes and 101 rounds to do so. The Leeds man's career came to an end when he was beaten by twenty year old Jem Massey at Ferry Moor in 1844. Smith achieved fame by beating a fighter named Russell in 1842. Fought for £50 aside and lasting 24 minutes, the fight proved fatal for Russell and Smith and his second, Sheffield boxer Joe Lowe were convicted. After serving one month in prison he had two quick victories over Alec Biggs and Patsy Cropley and then had a great win over a fighter called Evans in a match arranged at £50. His downfall came a year later when he took on a much heavier opponent in Kent and conceded inside two hours.

In 1838 the first move to clean up the sport had arrived with the London prize fight rules which forbid kicking, gouging, butting and insisted the seconds kept out of the ring. The next significant occurrence was the adoption of the Queensberry Rules, which were conceived in the 1860s and brought in nearer the end of the Century. The new rules, which made the bare fist fight illegal drove the prize fight further underground, although it would be a long time before it died out completely. A barefist fight at Temple Newsam in 1892 proved fatal to one of the participants, William Asquith. Robert Rothery was arrested and charged with manslaughter after Asquith died after failing to regain consciousness after a prizefight lasting twenty minutes. The public prosecutor stated that if it could be proven that excessive violence had been used during the fight, the charge would be changed to murder. Travelling showman, William Wilson, who refereed the fight, revealed that Asquith had been keen for the fight to take place. He had challenged Rothery and had found money to back himself. He gave witness to the fact that the fight had been fought in a sporting manner and that when Asquith had fallen injured, Rothery had offered to shake hands with his opponent and indeed previous to the latter minutes of the fight he had organised through his second a collection amongst the crowd for his opponent. This incident co-incided with two more deaths in the same week and it was obvious if boxing was going to have any future; it would have to clean up its image.

Despite its tarnished reputation the sport flourished underground, but as the twentieth Century drew nearer, the days of the bare-knuckle era were limited. Though there were still isolated cases (in remote Pennine villages, it did not die out for a long while). Glove boxing became accepted and with Lord Queensberry's rules giving the sport a chance for legality and acceptance in a public mode the sport came indoors.

CHAPTER 2

Boxing and the Music Hall

T he popularity of boxing advanced with the visit to this country of several World Champions who appeared at many provincial theatres as part of a 'musical hall' entertainment. The acceptance of boxing by the musical hall proprietors was an encouragement to the sports enthusiasts who repeatedly ran into trouble with local authorities who outlawed boxing in several areas and refused permission for fights to take place. John L Sullivan, Jim Corbett, Bob Fitzsimmons, Peter Jackson and later Jack Johnson, all world famous names, toured the music hall circuit giving exhibition fights.

The Bradford music halls, peaking in popularity around 1890, had a visit by Peter Jackson, the coloured heavyweight champion, in 1892. Jackson, the first coloured fighter to achieve any eminence, had been unbeaten for the last four years and had beaten the best men in England as well as Australia and the United States. The world champion, John L Sullivan refused to fight a coloured man in the ring but while in the States in 1891, Jackson had fought a sixty-one round draw with Jim Corbett. Sullivan was knocked out by Corbett a year later to become the first World Heavyweight champion (modern times glove fight). Jackson made an appearance at the Star Music Hall (in Concert Hall Court, Manchester Road, opened in 1875 with a capacity of 1200). It was announced that owing to Jackson's enormous fee of £50 prices would be 2s 6d for boxes. 1s promenade and 6d in the pit. Jackson's three round exhibition with Jem Young which only lasted about five minutes altogether was

Peter Jackson.

Jem Mace.
The last of the great English knuckle-fighters.

criticised by the press who reported that Jackson's administered body blows looked like mere taps. Jackson was dead by 1901 dying of tuberculosis at the age of forty.

In the same year as Jackson's visit, the evergreen retired bare fist champion of the World, Jem Mace, opened a six nights' engagement at the Princess Palace, Leeds with Charlie Myers of Bradford, the amateur champion of Yorkshire and Lancashire as boxing partners. Mace, the father of modern scientific boxing, had a fighting career spanning thirty-five years. In 1890, two years previous to his Leeds visit, Jem had fought Charley Mitchell in a contest, which was billed as being for the heavyweight championship of England. Mitchell was formerly British champion but had lapsed the title while he was in America fighting John L Sullivan. Needless to say Mace, who was aged fifty-eight, was beaten easily. Jem was later to return to the area as an actor when he gave a performance of 'The Great Glove Fight' at the Bradford Empire in 1905.

At the People's Palace (same hall as the Star, changed its name to People's Palace in 1896, a few years later reverted to just Palace), in 1899, part of the week's music hall entertainment was provided by American, Jack Burke, who gave demonstrations of knockout blows of famous fights with his partner, Will Scott. Burke, whose claim to fame was from a fight he took part in, in New Orleans, which lasted 110 rounds and lasted seven hours and twenty minutes, was in England for a projected battle with Dick Burge.

As well as featuring touring exhibition matches, the music hall was one of the few venues that opened its doors to the sport in this transitional part of boxing history. The Jollity Vaudeville Theatre (Canal Road, opened 1891) became Bradford's first main boxing venue and was proud to announce in 1896 a visit by the world middleweight champion, Bob Fitzsimmons. Though born in England, Fitzsimmons had done all his boxing in Australia and America. The champion stayed at the *Talbot Hotel* and brought his own sparring partner, Dan Hickey, with him to star in a 2¹/₂ hour show which included sparring and ball punching. The show, which was held over two days, included sparring bouts featuring local boxers, Charlie Parkinson, Jack Coss, Billy Emmott, Harry Clarkson, Fred Hill, Alf Suffolk, Ted Atkinson and George Ewing. A purse of £20 was offered to anyone who could stand up against the champion in four, three-minute rounds. Needless to say, there were no challengers. Within a year, Fitzsimmons was World heavyweight champion and when he was over forty, he won the newly created World light heavyweight championship. Leaving him with a unique record of three world titles at different weights, now not the only man to do so, but still the only man to win the three heaviest divisions.

Wrestling was also featured on the Jollity bill, the sport becoming more popular than boxing on the halls. Canadian, James Morgan had previously issued a challenge in the local press, to wrestle or box any man in Bradford. He had also stated that he would match anyone at weight lifting. After wrestler, Ernest Roeber, had accepted Morgan's challenge, Johnny Sheldon, the Jollity's proprietor, quick to capitalise on the situation, included the fight on the Fitzsimmons bill. In a fight for a £10 sidestake in a contest using Greco Roman style, Roeber threw Morgan after fourteen minutes, although Morgan wasn't satisfied and clamoured for a return. On the second night of the show, a Mr Atlas, who was performing for the week at the People's Palace, took Morgan on and also beat him, and again Morgan was dissatisfied and refused to accept the decision.

Jim Peach, who was probably not a Bradford lad but was employed for many years at a local brewery, often told a tale about a music hall episode which he took part in. In his day Jim was the champion prizefighter of his county and was once matched against the champion prizefighter of England (possibly Jem Mace) who was giving an exhibition at Norwich. It was announced that the colossal sum of £5 would be paid to any man who could stand up to the champion for three rounds. Egged on by his pals, who thought Jim was on easy money, the challenger entered the ring. At the end of the first round Jim had taken sufficient and wished to give over but was encouraged by his cohorts. He gave it another go. After the second round Jim was beaten to the world. His second's comment that he was winning brought forth the remark, 'well, if I'm winning, God help the loser'. Half way through the third, the reluctant hero was knocked out.

The Jollity Theatre

Under the guidance of proprietor, Johnny Sheldon, the Jollity Vaudeville Theatre saw many memorable matches from 1893 to 1897 when the Jollity was demolished to make way for the Empire Stores. Paddy Mahoney was the Jollity's top attraction and his big money match for a fight, which was billed as for the 8st 6lb championship of England with London's Tom Turner, was the biggest fight to take place at the Theatre. Besides Paddy's fights there were several other matches that achieved notoriety for one reason or another.

A fight arranged between two Leeds boxers, J Stringer and S Parker for a stake of £100 plus a side bet of £50 using 4 oz gloves for the nine stone championship of Yorkshire ended in a fiasco. Parker forced the fighting and on the call of time at the end of the third round had downed Stringer, the 6-3 favourite for the second time. Simmonds, Stringer's second, rushed into the ring and the referee gave the match to Parker on the grounds that he had no right to be there. Simmonds left the ring under protest. Unquestionably Parker had won by appearance at this time, as Stringer was weak and groggy. Following on from the dispute, Simmonds gave notice that the stakes were not to be paid out, his contention being that he had a right to be in the ring because his man was not down when time was called. The argument carried through to a court hearing the following year when the two fight backers, John Coyle and James Johnson of Hunslet, and the Jollity's owner Johnny Sheldon of Union Street met in court to settle their differences.

For a long time considerable local interest was built up for a fight between Jem Carlin of Leeds and W Lister of Bolton who were matched for the Yorkshire and Lancashire championship. Half an hour before the time fixed for the start, a large crowd had assembled in readiness. At eight o'clock it was announced that the principals had failed to come to terms and there would be no contest. The reason being that Lister had weighed in a couple of pounds over the stipulated weight and Carlin's trainer refused to let his boxer fight.

In 1896 Martin Madden met J Baines of Leeds for the 8st 6lb championship of Yorkshire for a purse put up by Johnny Sheldon. Apart from Mahoney's fight with Turner, this was judged to be the best fight ever to take place at the Theatre. The result being decided when Madden's party claimed a foul, which was allowed against Baines for hitting his man when down, when it looked as if he was going to win. Wrestling was also one of Sheldon's fancies, often combining both sports on the same bill. Johnny's big coup was a wrestling match between an American named Ross and Tom Cannon of Liverpool, which was for £50 a side, and for the world championship in five styles. (Scotch, Cumberland & Westmoreland, Collar and elbow, Greco-Roman and Catch as Catch can). Cannon won the contest by three styles to two. The last fight at the venue was between John McDermott of Manningham and Arthur Illingworth of Brownroyd in November 1897.

CHAPTER 3

Paddy Mahoney, Bradford's First Glove Champion

The most popular boxer to ever appear at Johnny Sheldon's Jollity was Paddy Mahoney, the Broomfield youngster who, in the few years leading up to the end of the century, became one of the leading ring men in the North.

Arriving in Broomfield, (a rough area dominated by Irish immigrants at the bottom of Wakefield Road, going out of the Bradford centre and mostly bulldozed in a 1935 slum clearance), as a youngster from Liverpool, and quickly adapting to his new environment, it wasn't long before young Paddy was mixing with the Atkinson boys, Teddy and 'Sticker', the prize examples of the Broomfield breed. Supporting Teddy at local gymnasium bills, whilst still only aged sixteen, Mahoney was matched with full grown men, and after 'Old Peg Tops' (real name Tommy Cullen, Bradford's most prominent boxer of the post Brassey era (1840) to pre Mahoney (1890) had

Paddy Mahoney.
Bradford's first glove champion who visited the music hall in Bradford in boxing's early history.

been to see him and to give him the nod, a noted fighter from Newcastle called Gibson was set on as his trainer.

As one of the early Jollity bills, in December 1893, the sixteen-year-old Mahoney was an instant success when he beat Johnny McGowan. Charlie Parkinson had been on the same bill and a little later he matched Paddy and McGowan again at his gym in Osborne Street. There was a lot of interest in the return and with stakes of £10 a side bet and £10 purse, local trainers Gerry Gosney and Harry Hoyle were appointed judges. McGowan got his revenge but finished up worse for wear than the loser. After nothing between the fighters, Paddy went down twice in the fifth round and convinced the second punch was before he was ready to resume, the youngster 'blew his rag'. The action could have been at the railway cuttings in Mill Lane or at the back of the saw mill. Paddy threw McGowan to the ground and lost the verdict on a foul. Paddy and Teddy had a laugh about it afterwards and when the former went through to watch the Atkinson brother in action at Huddersfield, promoter Best had failed to find an opponent for Teddy. The two Broomfield lads agreed to box a four round exhibition. Nothing was held back, the twosome went hammer and tong, with the crowd on their feet. Best bunged them a couple more quid and the battle went a couple more rounds and ended with two of the broadest grins imaginable.

After several wins at Charlie's gym, a fight was fixed with Bowling's Barney Bell, who was considered to be a hard test for young Paddy. A swinging right hand connected in round two and Barney did not hear the bell for round three. To keep the customers happy, old stager, Billy Simpson, had to don the gloves for a few rounds with an amateur. Simpson, who had been Mahoney's second for the Bell fight, officiated Paddy's next fight at the Jollity two months later, when Mick Murphy of Leeds was the opponent for the eight stone championship of Yorkshire. Paddy, who was barely eighteen, but not overawed, took the championship by beating Murphy in the fifth round. It was a pleasing night all round, for Young Mahoney had a couple of bob on Teddy who repeated the youngster's win over Barney Bell. Several more wins at the Jollity, plus the shrewd backing of local publican, John Coyle, enabled the attention of promoters outside the area to be attracted.

Fred Hare, winner of several open competitions in London, or so his publicity said only lasted three rounds, so Sheldon and his cronies scratched their heads and came up with William Webster from Manchester. Easily Paddy's biggest pay night so far, the best attendance at the Jollity for weeks was gathered to watch a fight fixed at £100 (£50 purse and £50 a side bet). What they witnessed was 'the story of the torn glove, a case of irregular proceedings'. The betting at the start was 6-4 on Webster, Whilst the men were putting on their gloves, one of them was found to be torn and to this, the referee objected. The parties, however, decided to toss for the torn glove and eventually Mahoney won it. This incident proved to be the turning point of the contest, for as it proceeded the stuffing of the glove kept coming out. At the end of round nine, the glove was only about half full of padding and the referee decided to stop the fight.

An unwise move, the two fighters refused to take any notice and carried on with their battle. Whereupon the referee attempted to leave the building, but was prevented by the crowd who pushed him back into the ring. It was not everyday you fought for a hundred pounds and referee or no referee; Paddy was in front by a mile. Eventually the Police came to the rescue and under their escort, the referee left the ring and eventually the police interfered between the boxers and the contest came to an abrupt conclusion. After much haggling and shouting, the match was understood to be postponed and would continue at a later date. After the crowd had gone home, the referee returned to give the verdict a draw. Paddy and his handlers were choked, especially as the Bradford man was well on top on points, but as the fight was only halfway through there was no real way for a mind change.

The bonus was that Mahoney's performance against Webster did enhance his reputation, and in 1897, with his backer John Coyle, Paddy signed articles to fight for a £100 a side, plus a purse of £200 put on by the Stalybridge Gymnastic Club for a twenty round contest at 8st 4lbs against well known George Corfield. South Yorkshireman Corfield ran his own boxing school 'The Excelsior School of Arms' at Sheffield and only the previous year had fought Billy Plimmer for the bantam championship before a 5,000 crowd. Plimmer in most quarters was recognised as World champion and had returned from successful tours in America. The Mahoney versus Corfield encounter duly took place at Stalybridge Gymnasium in March 1897. The admission charges of £1 and 10s were well out of reach of Paddy's usual gang of followers but were acceptable to members of the betting fraternity who had spent the afternoon of the fight at Liverpool races. The bookies' odds at Liverpool were 6-4 on Corfield, but with the gathering of the clan from Sheffield, the odds altered to 5-4. Despite the high entrance charge, a good attendance saw Paddy put up a great fight only to lose on points. Corfield had been in a different class from Paddy's previous opponents; nevertheless the youngster came away with a lot of credit in his defeat.

In November of the same year came Paddy's big chance, for Johnny Coyle had secured him a fight with Tom Turner of London. The terms of the fight were a twenty round contest with 4oz gloves and a purse of £60. The Jollity prices were up to accommodate and the local lads had to dig deep for Johnny Sheldon was on to a winner. Sportsmen all over the country were willing to travel to see a fight which the backers had announced was for the 8st 6lbs championship of England. Turner came with the reputation of having beaten Jim Williams of London twice, but like Paddy he had lost last time out, Will Curley of Newcastle being the man to dent Turner's record. Coyle wanted his man out of the limelight and sent him to Huddersfield to prepare under Freddie Best. The two fighters were weighed in the presence of a Bradford *Daily Telegraph* representative at four o'clock and both scaled within the 8st 6lbs. Edward Plummer of *The Sporting Life* was engaged as referee, while among Turner's seconds was the celebrated Tom Causer and in Paddy's corner was Jem Carney from Birmingham, an ex World Champion claimant. In an all action fight, amidst tremendous cheering (never had the pawn shop in Wakefield Road done so much business, the Broomfielders had pawned everything they could get their hands on to get the ticket money to see their hero in his greatest hour) the referee announced that Mahoney had won on points and it was later revealed that Mahoney had won eleven rounds to Turners seven with two being drawn.

As was fashionable in the fight game, Paddy became proprietor of a hotel. Bradford's leading boxer took up residence at *The Ashley* in Manchester Road and before long it was a rival to John Coyle's nearby *White Swan* as a den for fighters and their hangers on. Restlessness soon set in and Paddy got 'itchy feet' to cash in on his win over Turner and follow the trend of fighters who had tried their luck in America. Top English boxers could be guaranteed fights and a trip across the water could be both challenging and rewarding. After arriving in Liverpool, prior to his intended departure to the States where he was intending to challenge anyone at 8st 6lbs in New York State, his backers, after making enquiries ascertained that boxing competitions in the States had been stopped for the time being. After a short deliberation he decided to look some relatives up in Ireland and chance the possibility of a fight or two. The Bradford hero was soon in action seconding in a fight in Belfast and then travelled through Armagh in search of a challenge and took part in a contest at Banbrook Hill.

In the next year or two on his return from Ireland, Paddy retired and went into a promotion partnership with his friend John Coyle. By 1899 Harry Clarkson had assumed Paddy's mantle as the leading fighter in the town (I say assumed because in all reality 'Sticker' Atkinson was the new king) and there was considerable newspaper talk of a fight between Mahoney and the 'new Pretender' with figures up to £100 a side often quoted. Whether Paddy took up the challenge has not been verified, but there was a lot of animosity between the two when Mike Goulding, a protégé of Paddy's lost a decision to Clarkson.

Paddy's son Jim followed him into the boxing game and after a short career as a fighter, Jimmy was for many years one of the leading referees of the North.

To conclude the Paddy Mahoney story there was a funny tale of an incident, which circulated for many years among the boxing fraternity. T E Riley, the columnist on The Bradford *Daily Telegraph* revived the story in 1920 in his weekly boxing column under the title of 'Paddy Mahoney's Great Race'. Apparently one night Paddy wandered into the 'Rat Pit' (nickname for the City Gymnasium Club, which opened in 1899 and which dates the story about the same time) whereupon he was approached by Dr Bradley, a boxing enthusiast and Will Thomas, a well known publican. Evidently the two men had engineered a surprise for the boxer and before he could sit down, the doctor asked him if he would have a fight. Mahoney, who was not in training in this period, asked how big the purse was and the doctor replied 'Oh, if you win you can have two pound'. Paddy agreed and told the organisers he would be ready in five minutes. The question of whom was to be referee or indeed who his opponent was or any arrangement of weights were obviously not related. On entering the ring, to Paddy's amazement his opponent was at least two stone heavier and looked fit enough to fight for championships. On realisation that he was engaged in a bigger venture than he had bargained for, Paddy quickly decided on a plan of action. One thing he had learnt hanging around Hardy Street was when you are fighting somebody bigger and heavier, it was vital to get in that first punch. The plan worked a treat and Paddy won with a first minute knockout. As he turned to face his conspirators, the unknown boxer picked himself up and darted from the steps leading to the pit. Mahoney immediately jumped over the ropes and gave chase. Through the passage into Ivegate, along New Ivegate and out onto Market Street ran this half-naked boxer, with the local hero in pursuit. Local sportsmen Will Reams and PC Anderson gave chase and by the time Paddy had got to Charles Street, Reams had caught him and prevented him from running further. The unknown boxer was last seen racing along Canal Road. It was never learnt what had become of him, but it was a fact, he never claimed his clothes from the Rat Pit.

CHAPTER 4

Teddy and 'Sticker' the Broomfield Breed

Long forgotten in Bradford, but contemporaries of the older Delaney brothers, heroes to the younger brothers including Jerry who were fed on tales of the 'Cock of Ripley' and his hard as nails, never say die brother and epitomisers of the term 'Broomfield Breed' were the Atkinson brothers, Teddy and Sticker, or to give the latter his Sunday name, Will.

Willie was an onlooker when Teddy enhanced his street reputation as a 'good little un' at the opening of the new gym in Hardy Street by putting away Jem Carlin of Leeds in round seven of a contest billed as for the 7st 6lbs championship of Yorkshire. Johnny Sheldon gave Teddy his chance in the 'curtain raisers' at the Jollity and amongst his best recorded wins were a six round decision over Barney Bell (hailing from Bowling, Barney's clout as the best fighter in the area had lost ground in his two round defeat by Paddy Mahoney. His loss against Teddy silenced his claim altogether) and on the night Mahoney beat William Webster of Manchester in a £100 fight, Teddy beat William Lister of Bolton in four rounds.

Teddy was soon on the road appearing at Fred Best's promotions at Huddersfield and at the County Athletic Club, Leeds, but of all Ted's fights the one that lived longest in people's minds was the one that nobody paid to watch. The week after Teddy had won the 7st 6lb championship; John Willie Rooke, a Bradford lad of some promise, challenged him. Rooke did not want a glove fight, he fancied himself to be Atkinson's superior at bare knuckles. Although the fight was not arranged for very high stakes, the word had come through Broomfield and there was plenty of local backing spread around Ripley Mills Field at midnight. The fight with the 'raw uns' had drawn the attention of a great number of Bradford sportsmen, several of whom carried lanterns to aid the moon. As per usual heavy betting was a strong feature and although it was never recorded who was favourite, it only took two rounds of five-minute action in each,

Sticker Atkinson versus **Jimmy Rowan.** Boxers in a fifteen rounds bout.

for Teddy to take the verdict. Halfway through the second round, the Broomfield man had closed one of Rooke's eyes and after he had spent the remainder of the round holding Atkinson in a clinch, Rooke had to retire with the referee having no difficulty in awarding the stakes to Teddy.

Unfortunately the story did not end on a happy note. The win wasn't popular in all quarters and two days after the fight, Teddy was arrested at his home in Slaters Yard and remanded on a charge of receiving stolen property.

When young Willie had thoughts of emulating his brother, Teddy would hear none of it and when the youngster came persistent he was taken outside and showed his brothers disagreement in a rough and ready way. However when Teddy became injured at work and was laid up for a while, young Willie, not much gone fifteen, seized his chance and entered an open competition at the 'Rat Pit' (City Gymnasium). When Teddy got wind he was astonished to learn his brother had not only entered a competition, he had won it. When it was known that the 'boxing heads' in the town were willing to take young Atkinson under their wing and besides keeping him, allow his mother a payment a week to recompense for lost wages, the convincing was over. After a couple of more competition wins, Willie had his first big fight when he topped the bill at the 'Rat Pit' in September 1899 against George Bridgemont of Leeds. With odds of 11-10 on Atkinson, the contest arranged at 7st 12lbs with £10 a side and a purse of £15 10s supplied by the club lasted until the seventh round when the referee stopped the fight in Will's favour. The result was a big shock for the heavyweight champion, Cock Foster who was Bridgemont's backer. Determined to get his own back, Foster roamed the county for a challenger and came up with Billy Dunn of Sheffield. Atkinson's money went up to £25 and five rounds later the referee lifted his hand as Dunn's challenge was over.

Next came the memorable contest at the St George's Hall in December 1899. Unbeaten in approaching a dozen fights, Will was now looked after by Fred Hayes. The cockney Hayes had arrived in Bradford a couple of years earlier to fight Mahoney at the Jollity and had stopped on. Promoted by the City Club and witnessed by a crowd of over 2000, the Bradford youngster barely seventeen was matched with Ike Waudy of Hull at 7st 6lbs for £60. It was an historic occasion. For the first time in Bradford boxing history, ladies were allowed to witness the action and there was a sprinkling of females in the audience. In a very even contest, Atkinson was judged the winner on points. A decision popular with the followers who had made the short journey from Wakefield Road to fill the cheap seats. Only later it was revealed that the Broomfield lad had suffered several knuckle breaks in the second round. It made one wonder whether there was something special in the water at the bottom of Wakefield Road for the youngster had boxed twenty, three-minute rounds, the majority in excruciating pain. No wonder his 'muckers' had nicknamed him 'Sticker'! They had turned out to see him fight and no way was he going to let them down. After his hand had healed, well known Bradford sportsman Johnny Braham and Will Thomas sponsored his next fight, which was for a total purse of £85. His opponent was T Ganley of Birmingham and the action switched to Leeds to the County Athletic Club. What a fight it was! Sticker could not stay on his feet. Thirty times he was reputed to have been decked in the first two rounds. (A newspaper report of the fight at the time quoted approaching thirty occasions, whilst an old timer reminiscing many years after also quoted thirty falls). There was no way Will Thomas was going to throw the towel in. Every time Thomas asked him 'How are you Sticker. Do you want to throw the towel in?' Sticker replied he was alright. The lad's eyes were badly lanced and he was having much difficulty in seeing. Despite the handicap things started to improve and amazingly, much to the relief of Thomas, whose money was at stake, the Bradford fighter began to wipe off the adverse balance of points against him. Showing the ring craft of a veteran Sticker completely turned the tables and as the fight went further, it was obvious Ganley had shot his bolt. By the ninth the referee stopped it in favour of Will. The character to carry on when on the brink of defeat and to reverse the course of the fight against all odds to complete a triumphant victory was the passport to richer pickings in the boxing hotbeds of both Liverpool and Birmingham. To put greater emphasis on the victory, his opponent Ganley later beat American Sam Kelly, and Kelly had beaten the world champion, Billy Plimmer.

Sticker's first appearance in the North East saw him win inside three rounds against C Smirke of London, but in his second fight in Newcastle he was beaten by Peter Todd of Morpeth, a decision Sticker was able to reverse when he made Todd look like a novice in the return at Leeds. When the Leeds County and Athletic Club reopened in 1903 after eighteen months closure, new manager, Harry Dorsey, went out of his way to get Sticker as top of his bill and Sticker didn't let the Leeds boxing fans down. In a contest for £25 a side and the entire gate receipts which Harry had agreed to put up less expenses, in what was adjudged the best fight seen in Leeds, Will knocked his opponent Brady out in the thirteenth round.

Favourite of the Leeds businessmen was their own 'Cockney Cohen' when the Jew boy had put away one of the Delaney brothers inside a round, it was agreed Sticker Atkinson was the man to restore local pride. Odds of 6-4 were on Will but sadly the fight proved disastrous and for the first time in his boxing career the Broomfield man was outed in the second round. In the three or four years leading up to the First World War, with over twelve years experience in the ring behind him, when it was becoming obvious that Broomfield youngster Jerry Delaney was a cut above most of the up and coming talent, Sticker was a second and mentor in most of his early fights.

After being Bradford's leading fighter for the majority of the first decade of the new century, there were still plenty of ring battles for Sticker. In September 1910, the Bradford *Daily Telegraph* reported that boxing was still on trial in the city, determined efforts to stop it by some of the authorities had only been partly successful, so there was great interest in the first boxing bill at Belle Vue Barracks. Residing in Manningham, Kid Kelly had earned his reputation as an army champion in India. The promoters looked no farther. Sticker's name on the bill was always likely to pull the punters and there wasn't a better 'trial horse' in the town for any aspiring champions. Atkinson gave the 'Kid' exactly the sort of fight he wanted. After ten hard rounds, Kelly could not tick Sticker's name off on his winning record, but it was generally agreed that if the fight had gone on any longer then the verdict would have switched in favour of Kelly. In Sticker's next fight there was another demonstration of the comeback. The arena was Leeds Olympic, the opponent Wolf Brosgal, a promising Leeds boxer. Four rounds into the fight, Sticker had a closed eye and had made several journeys to the canvas. It seemed all over. Brosgal looked a certain winner. In a decade in the ring and a boyhood in Broomfield, you learn a bit about survival and at the end of the fifteen rounds, the lads who had backed Sticker were able to crack a smile.

Over 1,000 crammed into the first promotion at Wyke Baths. The main bout for a purse of £26 plus a side bet of £25 was between Albert Smith and Will 'Sticker' Atkinson. Smith, a newcomer to Bradford, was only participating in his third fight, but what had made people sit up was his second fight, a win over the rated Charlie McGowan. There was only one answer when Messrs Hart and Bromberg sat round the table to discuss who could put 'bums on seats' for their first promotion. But wasn't Smith three stone heavier than Atkinson? It was recalled that Sticker had once weighed in at 8st 6lbs and won a ten stone open competition at Bower Street. There was no persuading Mr Atkinson if the money was right he would fight anybody anytime. The occasion became a 'roughhouse'. Smith won a disputed decision on points, but he knew he had been in a fight.

In 1911, Freckleton Wraith opened a new boxing venue at Thornbury. The hall, capable of holding 1,500 and named the New Bradford Sporting Club, had a short life but in its year long existence was the scene of some great contests. (Wraith changed the venue to a physical culture club promoting several combat sports including the local celebrity, the ball punching Miss Rena Britton. The second venture was short-lived and the hall soon became the Cosy Cinema). Only eighteen, but with growing credentials as a future champion, Leeds teenager, Joe Fox put his unbeaten record on the line against the evergreen Sticker at Thornbury. Young Fox looked good but despite some serious efforts in the later rounds, Sticker stayed on his feet. A decade of experience in ring craft told the story and a bitterly disappointed Fox was beaten on points. The handlers of Fox were quick to demand a return to their 'own midden'. Amazingly, it was learnt that Atkinson, from a fall early in the fight had broken two ribs and only his indomitable pluck had enabled him to keep the secret even from Fox until after the fight. When the two rivals met again later in the year at Carlton Hill Barracks in Leeds, Fox had come on in leaps and bounds. Much too fast for the older man, it still took him to round fourteen before Sticker was finished. When Fox made his next appearance in Bradford in five years hence, his Lonsdale Belt was on show for the Leeds man had become British bantam champion.

During 1914 Sticker became troubled with an ulcerated stomach and after enlisting in the forces he was discharged with infirmity, It was while back in Bradford he had not his last fight, but his last memorable one. A succession of wins against the cream of Bradford boxers had lifted the status of Tommy Rowan in Keighley to one of hero worship. The talk was that no Bradford man could stand up to the Keighlians' hero. Sticker Atkinson answered the cause and strangely enough he was the same age as Rowan who had not started boxing until the age of twenty-seven. Half Sticker's life had been in the ring and to say he would have never passed a pre-fight medical was an understatement. Taking part in some of the most brutal fights in the last fifteen years had really taken its toll and that was the reason he was fighting Rowan and not for the King. Rowan won a close decision and although there was great interest in a rematch, for Will was convinced the referee had been biased towards the Keighley boxer, the War saw there was no immediate rematch. Atkinson succesfully re-enlisted and reached the rank of sergeant, only to be discharged with the same complaint.

Never a quitter, he even fought again after the War, but it was impossible for him to make any serious attempt at a comeback. In 1921 when he was thirty-seven, the Bradford boxing public rallied round in an attempt to get together a sufficient sum to enable him to get the best medical advice and rest in a nursing home. It was a sad end that not only Sticker, but also many of the boxers like him finished up heroes one minute, down and outers the next.

CHAPTER 5

The Fighting Delaney's

O f the many boxing families to come out of Bradford, one family stands head and shoulders above the rest as the producer of an array of boxing talent which, in the years before the First World War, put Bradford boxing firmly on the map. The fact alone of producing six brothers who were capable of earning a living as professional boxers has probably only been rivalled once by the Moody family of Wales, who were reputed to have produced seven.

William Delaney had moved from Tipperary to Bradford in the 1870s, marrying Catherine Durkin in 1880 the couple moved into the Irish quarter of Broomfields giving birth, as Irish families seemed to do in those days, to thirteen children in twenty-three years.

The boxing bug began with the second eldest brother, Jack, who became a more than useful bantamweight. Boxing at the turn of the century he was a regular at the 'Rat Pit' in Ivegate. Billy (who boxed as Fred) and Jerry (younger than Billy by seven years) became national figures in the sport in the period up to the First World War. Sadly their Bradford appearances were limited particularly in the case of Jerry, Bradford's only boxer of world championship class who only appeared in the City in his very early days.

Frank, who was a year older than Jerry, appeared spasmodically. He fought a well remembered £20 aside with Kid Kelly, the Manningham based Army champion, and was reputed to have beaten Johnny Basham, the British champion in an unrecorded fight. Joe, a game little boxer, and young Fred carried the name into the 1920s. Young Fred did not reach the heights that the experts predicted (Jerry was a hard act to follow) and after a premature retirement he fought again in the 1930s and became the last survivor of the brothers.

Thirty years of boxing did not stop there, with fighting in the blood; members of the next generation carried on scrapping with probably the best known being featherweight, Tommy Madden, a nephew of the brothers.

Billy the Kid to Fred the Elder
The First Delaney to reach Fistic
Fame outside Bradford

'Peerless' Jim Driscoll, who carved his own niche in the annals of boxing as the finest exponent of the straight left, quoted on many occasions that if it wasn't for his impetuosity in the ring, 'Fred' Delaney would have been a serious contender for world honours.

The Delaney Brothers (Fred and Jerry).

Following the family tradition, in which fighting was always second nature, the young *Bradford Telegraph* newsboy was not 'long in long pants' when he made his first appearance in the ring at a Jonty and Bill Simpson promotion at Lee Street, off Thornton Road. Jonty presented the youngster a medal with a gold centre for his winning endeavour. Even at this age the fiery temper had earned him a hostile reputation with the rival West Bowling street gangs. After things had become so hot locally, that the coppers had complained of sore knuckles knocking on his family's door, it was decided that it might be a good idea to vacate town for a while and join brother Eddie who was working as a bell boy in Birmingham. For a while young Billy took a job as a marker in a billiard hall. Dark corners of smoke ridden billiard halls were haunts of the fighting brigade and before long Billy had joined a boxing booth and was touring the Midlands and Wales. A breeding ground for many champions of the era and sadly a refuge for many old timers long past their best, the boxing booth was a passport to the richer pickings available in public hall promotion. So before long Billy Delaney was boxing under the name of Fred Delaney. The new name suited and confusion was avoided for there was another Billy Delaney boxing around the Midlands.

Jimmy Driscoll was five years older than the young Delaney and the Bradford boxer could not have had a better cohort in his graduation onto the big money boxing circuit. Perhaps in more later

Fred Delaney. Hardman of the fighting Bradford family.

years, for the modernists Howard Winstone has made it a three horse race, but for the older and more conversant boxing enthusiast it is a straight choice between 'Peerless' Jim (the nickname has become as legendary as the man himself), and the then soon to come 'Mighty Atom', Jimmy Wilde as the greatest fighter to come out of Wales. After the booth period, Driscoll's official record began in 1901 and by the time he was matched against Fred four years later, the Welsh ring wizard had only been beaten by Harry Mansfield, but at the same time Jim had beaten Mansfield on three other occasions. Fred entered the ring as a cocky twenty-year-old and although he had done enough sparring with the Cardiff man, to think he knew the weaknesses, it was a master versus pupil confrontation. The master had given a lesson, but was not boxing a learning process? Fred had picked up plenty about dirty fighting in the streets of Broomfields, he had learned a trick or two in the booths, but he was the first to conceive and admit many times in his reminisces later, a hour in the ring with 'Peerless' was an invaluable experience.

Driscoll ruled the roost in the British featherweight ranks from 1906-1913, making a clean sweep of British, British Empire, European and World titles. He made a short comeback after the war in 1919 and was beaten by Charles Ledoux in challenging for the European bantam title. His third defeat in a seventy-one-fight career. His other defeat was against fellow countryman Freddie Welsh, the

British lightweight champion in a non-title fight in 1910.

During his exile in Wales, the Bradfordian earned a reputation as a crowd pleaser, for quite often the fiery temper would get the better of him. The crowd knew if Freddie was riled, the 'fur would fly' and though it did not always mean victory, an absorbing free for all of a scrap was assured. The one man that Fred could not nail was fellow Yorkshireman Johnnie Summers. Middlesbrough born Summers, who claimed the British featherweight title in 1906, was British lightweight champion from 1908-1909, a title he lost to Freddie Welsh before adding the British and British Empire welterweight titles to his bow from 1912-1914. Fred was only eighteen the first time he tackled Summers and their 1903 fight ended in a loss on points. Two years later Fred got a second chance and was beaten inside the distance. When he took a third crack at Summers, the North Yorkshireman was at his peak and although Fred performed well to last the distance, the Bradford man had openly bragged before the fight that there was no way he would not. Summers completed his hat trick.

By 1909 Fred's sojourn in Wales was over. The boxing boom had reached Bradford. Major public hall promotion was happening and who better to 'pack em in' than the local boy made good. Not only that, Fred had received glowing reports of his younger brother Jerry, who had already commenced the fistic inroads among the lightweight ranks, and who had fought the cream of the British feather and lightweight over the last seven years?

Jerry Delaney. Bradford lightweight champion.

Bradford Interlude

The week before Christmas 1910 saw the third boxing promotion at the Belle Vue Barracks (Sticker and Kid Kelly had fought on the first). With Fred promising the fight starved Bradford fans a Christmas treat, the chance to see Delaney's first Bradford

appearance for many moons created the interest promoter Tommy
Maher dreamed about. The press played their part, reporting that
Fred who carried the title, the nine stone champion of Wales, was in
strict training at the *Kings Arms* while his opponent Alf Wood was
doing his stint at *The Packhorse*. Alf was originally out of London but
had been Bradford based for a while. His best-recorded win had been
against Johnnie Summers, Fred's bogey man. A 'house full' sign went
up early in the evening, but as the minor bouts got through, the
sensational rumour got about that Delaney was refusing to box for the
£30 offered. Amid considerable excitement, Fred and his cronies who
included several brothers were seen to make their exit. With the hostile
crowd baying for blood, the red faced Maher had to climb in the ring
to explain that one of the lads (everyone knew who) had declined to
fight for the £30, which he had understood had been agreed to.
Embarrassing himself even further, poor Maher admitted he was a
novice at promoting and had not obtained the boxer's acceptance on
paper. In a step to calm things, Maher added he would offer another
fiver to the purse, during which Wood stepped into the ring and said
he was willing to go ahead for the original £30. The faces of the
remnants of the Delaney party that were at ringside were non-
committal. Meanwhile Freddie was relaxing in the dressing room, he
had promised the Broomfields party he would stand them a round or
two of Christmas drinks and his plan to get the 'brass' was going nicely.
One or two Broomfielders were planted in the crowd and when it
looked like the officials might have a riot on their hands, Messrs Alf
Barraclough and Tom Priestley donated £5 each, making a £45 purse,
which was sufficient to make Freddie leave his dressing room. Before
the fight, Fred had been the 'local hero' but now the crowd's allegiance
had switched to Wood and they wanted the cocky blighter's block
knocked off. Fred had learned about 'geeing up' in his booth days and
although Wood looked to be doing well in the early stages; the money
backed in favour of Delaney was safe. By the time it had come to round
fifteen, Wood was unable to take any more punishment.

The flanker worked by Fred did not go against him and Delaney
was top of the bill again at the next Barracks promotion. The
promoters had learned by their mistakes and although prices were up
to accommodate the fiery character, 3,000 were crammed in to the
venue. Many were hoping to see the 'cocksure bandit' get his
desserts. Nobody dare breathe in, in case someone pinched the space
and there were even spectators hanging off the iron roof supports.
Fred took the fight at £80 plus £50 side bets which made the fight
worth £180. The opponent was Albert Smith and the novelty was

Smith was a Welshman. So here we had a Welshman who had moved to Bradford some time ago to learn to box, and a Bradford man who had moved to Wales to box and was the Welsh nine stone champion. Smith proved durable, but there was never any chance of an upset and Fred was able to put on a demonstration for brother Jerry, an interested spectator in Fred's corner. For the first time the two brothers had fought on the same bill and before Fred's points win, Jerry had so outclassed and demoralised his opponent, Young Wilkinson of Brighouse that the youngster gave up after one round.

By now the two brothers were sparring and training together on a regular basis at local rooms in Walton Street and eye witnesses were able to recall later that there was never any holding back when the two brothers were in the same ring together. As the younger brother, Fred (the real Fred) was able to relate, much later in life,

A friend of mine once told me that he had watched boxing all over, but he had never seen anything as hard, and two boxers put in so much as when watching Jerry and Fred sparring.

Fred was in vociferous mood when he, along with Sticker, was in the corner for Jerry's first big fight which was against Fred Blakeborough at the Coliseum Ice Rink in Toller Lane in 1911. Jerry recorded a points win against his great Bradford rival but Fred's behaviour nearly unstuck all the good work. Referee M Murray, who at the time was editor of 'Boxing', commenting on the fight years after, related that Fred seriously jeopardised Jerry's chances by persisting with a stream of advice at the top of his voice. Only after he stopped the fight and warned that Jerry would be disqualified, did he quieten down.

World Tour - London, America, Wales again and Australia
With his backers pressing his claim to fight anyone at 9st 2lbs, Fred made several journeys to London to fight in 1911 and 1912. In a fight at the Sporting Club in April 1911 Fred was matched against Wally Pickard of Haymarket. Both men had a reputation as scrappers and several times the referee had to warn both fighters to box cleanly or they would both be out of the ring. Affairs lasted until the eighth round when a series of heavy punches put Pickard's 'lights out'! Fred's fight at the South London Palace of Varieties started in disaster when his opponent Kid Davis, an American who had been unbeaten whilst living in France put him down twice in the first round. During the rest of the fight, Fred had to get his head down and 'work his socks off' at a furious pace to take the verdict on

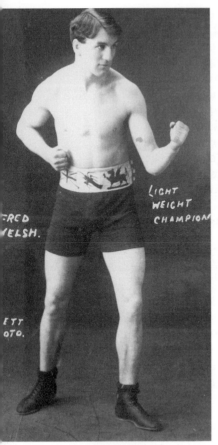

Fred Welsh. The
Lightweight Champion.

points. In January 1912 he made an appearance at Dick Burges 'The Ring' in Blackfriars (nicknamed the working men's boxing club, the Sunday afternoon venue was destroyed by a German bomb in the second world war), where he recorded a knockout win over Bert Black in the ninth round.

During 1912, Fred along with his brother Jerry who had already started to make a name for himself in the northeast decided to follow the current trend among top British fighters and try their luck in America. Driscoll, Summers, Welsh and Matt Wells who had taken the British lightweight title from Welsh (Welsh regained it in November 1912) had all tested the water in the States and the lure of greater fame and fortune saw them sail west. Fate played a hand for had they sailed when they had originally intended to, they would have been on the *Titanic*, and a hold up meant sailing later. Poor old Fred. His stomach did not agree with the sea and the elder brother spent the entire journey on sick parade. Fred wrote a letter home saying they were staying in Philadelphia and that they had given a rather unique performance by boxing in the bedroom of a banking millionaire. The bedroom had been made into a gymnasium for the occasion and it was especially pleasing as there were over 500 pro-boxers in Philadelphia and the Delaney brothers had been the first pair invited to box at Mr Biddles home. Biddles was so impressed that he engaged them to box at a private party given afterwards. Though he was still unwell, Fred managed to put up good performances in the two matches he took part in. A scheduled fight with Tommy Murphy was cancelled and so keen to fight was Fred, he took on a substitute Sam Robidean who was eleven pounds heavier. After he had beaten Tommy Langdon in Philadelphia and Jerry had put up a good performance against Bobby Scanlon in New York, the brothers received enthusiastic coverage in the local American papers but the possibility of staying on ended when Fred, who had been unwell for most of the trip, decided to head home. The elder brother

Jerry Delaney, D.C.M., with the well-known trainer, Billy Purvis, Charlie Costello and Llew Roberts.

had been unable to keep anything down whilst at sea, the American food did not agree with him either, and the thought of staying on was not as persuasive as his mam's own flat cake and Irish stew.

Back in England again in 1913, Fred returned to the scene of some of his earlier triumphs when he had several important fights in Wales. There were two great tussles with Fred Dyer, the Welsh welterweight champion at Cardiff Skating Rink. Dyer, who had also been in America in 1912 had looked invincible at one time and had an unbeaten two year period in 1908-1909 totalling almost fifty fights. Freddie Dyer had another career as well in show business as a singer and a song at the end of a Dyer victory was a standard request in Wales. The Welshman had studied under Dame Clara Novello, the famous singer and mother of Ivor. Dyer won the first meeting on points and public demand was so much for a return that the two rivals met again three months later. Fred had complained that he had to concede too much weight at the first meeting, but because conditions had now changed and he was the challenger, there were no grumbles from Fred having to travel from Bradford to Dyer's own backyard. (About this stage of his life, Fred had left his Wakefield Road roots to live in the posher Falmouth Avenue, or as one pundit remarked 'They would be better renaming it "Foulmouth Avenue" now that Fred had moved in'). The return unofficially described by the organisers as for the lightweight championship of Great Britain (Freddie Welsh was champion) was arranged for £200. This time Delaney gained his revenge with a handsome points win. In November 1913 Freddie Dyer's dual role took him to a week's booking at the Bradford Empire and as an extra bonus Freddie Delaney sportingly came along at the end of the singer's performances and gave an impromptu sparring session. When the Welshman introduced Fred onto the stage he made a big fuss stating that Fred had been the only boxer who had really beaten him. The two rivals were in action the following March at Cardiff, this time Dyer was the victor over twenty rounds. At the same venue in Cardiff during the latter part of 1913, Fred met Dai Roberts of Caeraa who had recently beaten Arthur Evans for the Welsh lightweight championship. Fixed at £200 this was to be the eliminator for a fight at the National Sporting Club for the English championships. Roberts had the stronger finish and took the verdict in a fight, in which Fred fell foul of the referee and was reprimanded, several times for wrestling. Earlier in that year, Joe Jagger who was Fred's backer had guaranteed him £100 to try and obtain a fight with Freddie Welsh for the lightweight championship and the Lonsdale Belt. (Although time has not been kind to Freddie Welsh and he never had the lasting fame of his contemporaries Driscoll and Wilde, boxing historians would class him in the same breath and would argue whether there has ever been a better defensive boxer from this country among the lighter weight divisions. In a career spanning seventeen years Welsh took part in 168 contests, he was British and European lightweight champion 1909-11, undefeated British lightweight champion 1912-1919, Undefeated British Empire and European lightweight champion 1912-14, World Lightweight champion 1914-1917. The first outright winner of a Lonsdale Belt. Welsh was only beaten four times, twice in the championship ring, once early in his career and for the last time in an ill-fated comeback. Half his fights were in America; thus accounting for the eighty-one no decision fights on his record). The National Sporting Club (the club controlled all title fights at the time) manager A F Bettinson replied that if the fight were to take place at least £200 would be needed. Jagger answered him by saying the money would be found but before any arrangements became concrete, Fred's title hopes were dealt a bad blow when Sapper O'Neill knocked him out in five rounds at Liverpool Stadium.

In turn 1914 was a mixed year for Fred. He beat Bill Johnson who was the strong favourite at Sparkbrook Stadium, Birmingham, Winnipeg O'Brien the lightweight champion of Manitoba at Bolton, but he lost to Eddie Beattie at the Scottish National Club.

Ironically whilst Fred's hopes of fighting Welsh were getting increasingly slimmer, brother Jerry had hit the headlines at the National Sporting Club in London and there was talk of the younger Delaney brother being matched with the World Champion, that is if he could be enticed from the lucrative American circuit. These frequent training bouts between Fred and Jerry which had so often developed into real slams that any promoter would have been proud to put at the top of his bill, had been the platform of Jerry's four year rise from Broomfields to the top of the British lightweight ranks building up an unbeaten fight record on the way. With the country at war the brothers, prior to Jerry being drafted abroad with his regiment, were in demand locally starring in open-air exhibitions and music hall appearances to raise money for the war effort. With over a decade of ring experience coupled with his background in Wales, Fred had first hand knowledge of the Champion Welsh. He knew about the champion's habit of hitting with one hand and holding with the other when the referee was on the blind side, he knew about his method of slipping his head under his opponents chin to give him a mild butt, he also knew about Welsh's remarkable stamina, his ability to conserve himself during stages of the fight and he knew when Welsh was at his most dangerous. Despite working on the moves with Freddie imitating Welsh's stance and methods, the dream never came to fruition. Welsh stayed on in America and Jerry's draft came through and ended in 'No Mans Land' in 1915. Jerry's death, some of the other Delaney brothers still missing in France, Fred felt the need to leave the intensity and although others were quick to rebuke, had not Welsh and all the other top British boxers in America and Australia heard about the Kaiser?

The boxing boom was on in Australia. Tom McCormick, Johnnie Summers, Llew Edwards and Fred's old mate Freddie Dyer who fought Les Dancy for the European middleweight title in Sydney, had been there and when the favourable comeback reached Fred he decided to try for himself. One of his final fights before sailing to Australia was at the Scottish National Club where Fred going through weight problems had to pay a forfeit for being two pounds over the stipulated weight of 10st 2lbs.

The fight in which Fred Delaney was probably most remembered for actually took place in 1915, the year before he departed down under. A Romanian middleweight, Costica Alexandrescu, visited this country and after he had licked two of our top boys in Gus Platts and Tom McCormick (Platts was a future European champion whilst McCormick after his 1914 win in Sydney against Waldemar Holberg had claimed the World welterweight title). Fred was given the honour of restoring British pride when he was put in with the Romanian at West London Stadium. The European looked as if he would be more at home in the wrestling ring and it soon became understandable how McCormick had got himself disqualified in his encounter. Now Fred knew all about roughhouses, he had a few in the ring and plenty outside in his time and when Alexandrescu began pushing and mauling Fred all over the ring, the ringsiders who knew Fred were counting the seconds before the time bomb went off. Fred surprised a few that night and he stuck to boxing. The Bradford man had weighed up his opponent in a breath and after refusing to be agitated into a brawl he gave Alexandrescu a boxing lesson for the rest of the fight. The one big mystery afterwards was how the referee had made it a draw, when general belief was Fred had won by a mile.

By the time Fred had left for Australia in 1916 he was up to 10st 7lbs. During his spell in Australia, Fred had a couple of fights with Frank O'Connor. In the first he was well beaten and his seconds had to throw in the sponge in the seventh round. The return, which took place at Sydney Stadium, came to an end in the tenth round when O'Connor was floored after some infighting. Fred had insisted he had an off day in their first fight and had put a few bob on himself in the re-match. To the delight of the astonished onlookers, the referee gave the verdict to O'Connor declaring that Delaney had committed a foul with his knock out punch. Whilst in Australia Fred joined the Australian army and quickly became their welterweight champion. A stop came to his army career when he joined the Great War and was gassed and wounded at Vimy Ridge. Invalided out of the force Fred returned to his Bradford roots, where after a brief convalescence he attempted to return to his boxing career. To be fair to Fred he was now approaching middle thirties and was nowhere near the same boxer after his ordeal in the War. Consequently he lost fights to boxers who would not have stood an earthly a couple of years earlier. Since his teenage years boxing had been his only trade and although Fred at times had fingers in other pies he had to turn to the old Bradford trade of 'a bit of this and that' to supplement his boxing income. Although he was still a name locally and a fighter whose name many of the young up and coming boxers wanted on their winning records, Fred's fight fees were nothing like he was earning before the war. And Fred had other problems; he had married in 1917 and subsequently had two children to support.

Old Fred and Young Fred

Fred returned to fight action in his home town in 1917 when Edwin Holloway, who was to become Bradford's leading promoter of the twenties, because of the unavailability of the regular boxing venues due to use by the military, and anxious to revive the sport booked Fred to fight a catchweight contest against Bob Spencer of Belfast who claimed to be the welterweight champion of Ireland, in a tournament held at the Palace Music Hall as part of a Saturday matinee. The home crowd was touting for a Delaney win and the majority of spectators had thought Fred had done enough to do so. The referee did not see it that way and gave his decision a draw. Fred did not win his next Bradford fight either. The ring veteran was disqualified for hitting low against Driver Symonds. The rumpus not going down too well with the watching councillor F Liles and his guest, Sir John Maxwell, Chief of Northern Command.

By now the younger Delaney brother, the real Fred, had started his career as Young Fred Delaney, the latest boxing brother had not been born when Jack Delaney had hung up his gloves and had been a youngster of nine when he had been taken from Granby Street to watch Jerry in action at Leeds, the only time he ever saw him box. As he had with Jerry although no way near with the same vigour, Fred taught his brother the rudiments of the game.

The formation of a boxing academy, just above Broomfield at Walton Street off Hall Lane, premises which had been previously used by the Delaney's for training gave local boxing a boom just after the War. Both Belle Vue Barracks and Windsor Hall (up to the beginning of the War the venue had been known as the Central Baths Hall, then changed its name to the Kursaal, and then because the new name was considered German within a year was re-titled Windsor Hall) promotions had suffered severely with cancellations and were often criticised for putting on shows which were a travesty of the ones advertised in the press. The small club type promotion, obviously in the pocket range of the less well to do were of particular encouragement to the lesser lights in the sport who usually struggled to get backers to appear on the bigger promotions and so consequently were willing to appear for small purses or enter competitions for medals. The small club was packed out regularly during 1919. At the club's opening tournament Young Fred made one of his first appearances easily outclassing J Gillespie. Wins over Clarence Booth (Huddersfield) and Johnny Harrison of Chorley followed, and Young Fred began to catch the eye of Edwin Holloway.

When boxing had started to pick up the threads again after the War, there was a movement to popularise open air boxing in the city. An experimental tournament held at Valley Parade in 1916 had proved successful so Holloway revived outside fighting in the summer of 1919. Alfie Hebblethwaite was reputed to be a champion in the making. Only a year or two ago the internationally famous referee Eugene Corri had given him the title 'Boy Champion of England' at the Variety Club, London. When the year younger seventeen-year-old Young Delaney began to earn a similar reputation, Holloway had a natural billtopper for his Valley Parade promotion.

The fight was fixed for a £45 purse and £50 a side and was advertised for the bantamweight championship of Yorkshire. The Delaney pedigree helped swell the crowd to over 6,000 and although the eighteen-year-old Alfie had taken part in a colossal number of fights for someone so young, Delaney's punching created havoc.

The referee was forced to intervene after several knockdowns. Alfie's backers, frightened that the golden goose had died, complained that they weren't happy with the alleged weight of Delaney. Old Fred had been around too long to fall for that line. Money in pocket meant 'two fingers' to any re-weigh!

After a successful series of summer tournaments, promoter Holloway opened his winter season at the Windsor in October. When his bill topper, Dick Moss v Fred Blakeborough had fallen through, the wily Edwin came up with the 'old campaigner' versus the young up and coming challenger. 'Driver' Harris was now approaching forty. Originally from London way he had found his way to Bradford after the War and he had opened a popular gymnasium in Brownroyd. You could not take it away from the ageless 'Driver'. He had few equals in the town at the dawning of the twenties, but what got up people's noses was the southerner's arrogance. If he had worked a comfortable points margin lead instead of pressing on he would be content to step aside and walk round the ring, smile at friends in the audience and produce his party trick when playing to the crowd, a stupefied grin when making his opponent miss. Young Fred had already had Windsor Hall experience having fought on Holloway's Spring programme, stopping Billy Norfolk of Leeds in four rounds and Young Calvert of Elland in two rounds. In today's boxing scene, a cagey manager would have kept an eighteen-year-old newcomer away from someone as experienced and considerably heavier as Driver (about the time Driver had two great battles with Fred Blakeborough in Bradford. Both fights went the distance and drew capacity crowds. Blakeborough won both but he was among the top three or four lightweights in the country). To his credit Young Fred survived a first round knockdown and though he would have probably lost on points the man who was twice his age made sure by knocking Fred down in the last round. On reflection in later life on the day he lost his unbeaten record, Young Fred had no memory of the fight. 'I don't remember the fight to this day' he recalled, and from a slip in the fourth round he added: 'I must have had concussion and fought automatically to the end'.

A month later it was the older Fred who stepped into the limelight at Holloway's November promotion. The occasion proved one of the most enduring contests of his well over a hundred fights. Seaman Cox from Wigan, the welterweight champion of the Navy took the points. The decision did not go down too well in the Delaney camp who invaded the ring on one occasion to claim the fight on a foul. The Broomfield bunch demanded a re-match. 'Cox would not have lived two minutes with Fred in his pomp' they retorted. But Fred was not in his pomp. Two decades of boxing, a War injury from which many thought he would never enter the ring again, had taken their toll. Fred got his re-match three months later at the Windsor. The second fight turned out another gruelling affair. Fred never quit in his life and there was no way he would surrender in front of his own lot. Fred took quite a pounding; he lasted the course but paid the penalty of a badly lacerated face. At least the Wakefield Road brigade had something to cheer that night. Young Fred on the comeback trail beat Kid Hewitt in four rounds.

Old Fred's career was in the last cycle when he helped Ellis Boldy out at one of his open-air promotions at Greenfield (Dudley Hill). Kid Lees of Oldham had been unbeaten at Boldy's earlier promotions and although the youngster was much too fast for Fred, the two fighters had another battle with the rain and wind. There was a touch of the 'chip off the old block' when Young Fred showed a facet of the elder brother's temper when he threw Liversedge's

George Senior out of the ring to earn a disqualification on another Boldy bill.

Dickie Metcalfe of Girlington had been one of Bradford's top boxers around 1913. Fred, of course, at the time was travelling all over the country to meet rated boxers, so consequently their paths had never met in the ring. Metcalfe and his handlers had been spectators at Fred's defeats against Cox and conflict between the Girlington party and the Broomfield brigade had led to a challenge being thrown out. Metcalfe, on the comeback trail, wanted the thirty-five year old Fred on his record and Fred could not resist a challenge and another pay night. When Fred Blakeborough pulled out of his scheduled fight with Charlie Hardcastle, the former champion, the crafty Holloway was quick to substitute the needle match on the bill. Although the respective parties reached the fever pitch of excitement the two boxers might as well have been fighting in the back streets outside. Science and boxing expertise 'went out of the window' as the fighters took part in a brawl that would not have disgraced a Wild West Saloon. The referee had to intervene repeatedly as 'the lot went in'. Low hitting and head butting were standard practice before the referee decided that enough was enough and disqualified Metcalfe in round seven for a low punch. The Girlington party was furious, having reckoned on easy money betting against the ageing Delaney. Despite vigorous appeals to bring a doctor into the ring to examine Delaney to determine whether a foul blow had been struck, the referee was adamant the decision was final. The Girlington boys did not like it, but one look at the couple of 'boys in blue' at the back of the hall was enough to deter any more excitement.

Not long after that Fred wisely announced his retirement and as a farewell to one of Bradford's greatest boxers, a benefit was held in his honour at Windsor Hall in late 1920. Organised by Holloway, the highlight of the evening was an appearance of Fred's old pal from the days of 'Old Peerless' himself, Jim Driscoll. The Welsh master gave a three round exhibition with Fred Blakeborough. (Sadly Jim passed away with pneumonia in 1925 at the age of forty-five and in a series of strange quirks of fate befalling Welsh champions: Freddie Welsh died in 1927 penniless at forty-one; the former British bantam champion, Billy Benyon who accumulated 192 contests including ninety-one defeats died from a mining accident in 1932 aged forty-one having spent over half his life in the ring; Tom Thomas the British middleweight from 1906-1910 had only been thirty-one when he had passed away with pneumonia fever and flyweight Percy Jones the World flyweight champion in 1914 died in 1922 aged only thirty).

Joe Delaney, who had been a frequent lower down the bill performer at the Windsor, beat Young Harris and Young Fred made it a family double when in a scheduled ten rounder he sent Joe Walsh of Oldham crashing out of the ring in the first round. Holloway even had Delaney's old enemy Driver Harris on the bill. The catcalls that greeted his appearance changed to cheers when in an exciting bout Driver had to retire in the eleventh round against Kid Lees. A fortnight later it was the turn of another of Fred's Welsh pals to grace the Windsor floorboards when Jimmy Wilde gave two three round exhibition rounds. The two opponents were bigger and heavier men and Wilde brought howls of laughter from the spectators when, for a period he stood in the middle of the ring arms by his side while his opponent found it impossible to even land a blow. When Young Fred's opponent failed to turn up Walter Stanton of Leeds, who had put up the better show of the two exhibitors, stepped in. Wilde took over as referee and in a bout that was spoiled by too much clinching, Jimmy gave the verdict to Young Fred. A decision that was not too popular with the crowd especially as it was well known that in Wilde's early days, the elder Fred Delaney had helped sponsor him.

There were several more fights for Young Fred in the early twenties but the one that outlived all the others in memory was the re-match with Driver Harris. The rivalry in the Delaney and Driver Harris camps led Mr Ainley, a well known business man in the town, to book Belle Vue Barracks to stage a contest between the zealous competitors. Both camps had deposited a big sidestake and a full house was expected. Young Fred had put weight on recently and although he had lost the first meeting he was considered by many to be the favourite. Ainley appointed the old champion Paddy Mahoney as his manager, but alas the old Broomfield stager was not really up to the job. The first major complaint was that many of the promotions patrons had paid five shillings for the ringside tickets and had found their seats occupied by a rough element and alternative seating accommodation could not be found. The non-numbering on the seats which should have corresponded with the numbered tickets led to a fracas amongst the audience which led to a seething atmosphere. It was apparent that great deals of people were in the hall without paying (when the tale was told a while afterwards, it was suggested that the Broomfield Brigade had been let in by a side door for a back hander.) The failure to produce the customary programme for sale supposedly was to let the management off the hook over the non-arrival of fighters and the other problem was that the bell could not be heard more than a yard away from the ring. The extreme needle between Harris and Young Fred came to an explosive end in the sixth round when Harris was disqualified. Harris had had the better of the fight and it was quite apparent that Delaney was in difficulties by the sixth round. It looked all over, when during the round, Delaney fell to the floor. As the crowd stormed to the ringside it was difficult to see what had happened. It was said that Harris rushed forward and hit Fred as he was rising and put him down again. Immediately after the Delaney camp swarmed into the ring claiming a foul as the crowd surged towards the ring with the impression that Driver had won. It did not go down too well with the Brownroyd party, when the referee announced he had stopped the fight as Harris had been disqualified. Bottles and broken chairs went through the air; fights began between the rival factions with the referee Tommy Cullens the most unpopular man in the place having to seek refuge. The general feeling was (but not amongst the Broomfield brigade) that the Delaney seconds were at fault in entering the ring whilst the fight was still in motion and the referee should have refused to give a decision. Poor Fred could not remember his first meeting with Harris and he was stretchered out in the second, although revenge was sweet, at least for the lads who had put money on him.

There were still a few more fights for Joe, but for Young Fred boxing was over. Three years later in 1924 professional boxing in Bradford suffered a severe setback. The Syd Pape versus Ted Kid Lewis fight at the Windsor Hall was considered so brutal that it was six years later before the city magistrates would give another licence to permit the sport. The arrival of the club boxing boom in the early thirties, when there were nearly as many clubs putting on weekly shows as picture houses and Walton Street and the Farmyard in Bowling Back Lane were the top venues. Young Fred was tempted back into the ring, but like a lot of comebacks it did not last long.

The same year the Bradford boxing ban commenced, Old Fred got a job with the Bradford and District Newspaper Co Ltd. In the thirties he moved to Donisthorpe Street in West Bowling and was still living there and working for the paper when he died after a long illness in 1949 aged sixty-four.

The Tragedy of Jerry Delaney
From Newsboy to the National Sporting Club

The finest of the boxing Delaney brothers was undoubtedly Jerry. No disrespect to any later boxers who fought for titles, but Bradford has never produced better. The great tragedy of Jerry Delaney is that not only did the Great War rob Bradford of the chance of a world title holder, but it stopped us from knowing how great in the sport Jerry could have become in fulfilling the expert predictions made about him.

After leaving St Anne's School in Broomfield, the youngster from Granby Street followed Billy's (Fred the Elder) footsteps into a job as a newspaper seller of the Bradford *Daily Argus*, and it was not long before young Jerry was following in his brother's footsteps in another direction. Broomfields was full of fighters of one sort or another and Jerry was only following a tradition of hungry fighters by donning the boxing gloves. When the local awareness of his potential came into being, there could not have been a better right hand man than his brother Fred. In his ten years in the ring Fred had fought the best lightweights in the country and it's a documented fact of the time that some of the hardest fights in Jerry's five year career were in the training ring with brother Fred. After winning his first fight in spectacular fashion by a first round knockout, the power of Jerry's right hand punching guaranteed him a run of quick wins and by 1911 Jerry had followed in the footsteps of Paddy Mahoney and Sticker Atkinson by becoming the new idol of Broomfield. (Fred never became a street idol in the same sense because for a big percentage of his fistic career he was not around).

Whilst Jerry's reputation was quickly growing Bradford had another young man with similar aspirations in Fred Blakeborough, who had made a name locally with a win over Curly Osborne of London who was billed as the 7st 6lb champion of England and a winner of over 200 contests. As a result of a series of challenges between the two fighters in the press, the two youngsters met at the Coliseum Rink, Toller Lane in a fight fixed at £75 for the winner. Despite a drenching night there was a tremendous attendance. 'Bus loads' had come through from around Granby Street and as soon as the doors had been opened the reserved seats had been rushed with the tickets on them conveniently left under the seats. Fred's seconds were Manningham based fighter Alf Wood, Fred's father Ben and his brother Will (later killed in action in 1915). In Jerry's corner he had Fred, Sticker and Sam Leach. The referee was M Murray, the editor of 'Boxing'. To the onlookers it appeared a very close contest with Jerry edging it. There was no doubt in Murray's mind, on his card Jerry had won twelve rounds. Fred four, and four even. As the Delaney camp went their happy way back to Broomfields, no one had an inkling that they had seen Jerry's last big fight in Bradford.

The following year the lads who earned their living from boxing suffered a blow when the Chief Constable in the City announced that no licences to allow professional boxing in Bradford would be given. The Delaney's who had at one time been based at *The Castle*, and later moved to Tom Maher's *Packhorse* were even stopped training rights. The ban lasted until March 1914. Unable to fulfill his ambitions in his hometown Jerry moved to the Northeast where he boxed a draw at South Shields with Johnny Robinson in a match for £25 a side. Jerry was not alone in the Northeast, the Blakeborough brothers found work there and with all three of them around the lightweight range, they were able to 'compare notes' on opponents.

Despite barely two years experience, the fame and fortune of America was too big a 'carrot dangler' to resist. His brother's illness curtailed the Stateside trip and Jerry's only appearance in a proper fight was a thrilling six round no-decision contest against Bobby Scanlon in New York. With good press reviews there was the chance of staying on with every promise of making good. Family loyalty came first and with the ban still on in Bradford it was back to the North East on his return for Jerry.

Back in action in Newcastle, Jerry took up where he had left off by stringing together several victories. Among the fights he won at St James's Hall were a decisive points win over Barney Kirk of Barrow, a similar result over Billy Galley of Wrekenton and an eighth round knock-out win against Harry Sterling when odds of 11-8 were laid on Jerry. It was whilst he was in the Northeast he had a notable victory over the Frenchman Eugene Volaire. The Broomfielder outboxed his opponent for five rounds before falling to a left hook, as he was about to finish his man. The blow had caught Jerry flush on the jaw and only Yorkshire grit enabled him to rise off the canvas to beat the count. While the Frenchman pursued him around the ring looking to land the killer punch, a brilliant display of defensive boxing which brought the crowd to their feet, saw that by the end of the next round Jerry's sheer pluck was 'swinging the pendulum' back. In the next two rounds Volaire was punched to a standstill before he 'fouled out' to earn a seventh round disqualification. (Fouling out, as the term was known, was a facet of boxing. When a boxer was on the verge of being beaten, he deliberately earned a disqualification which did not look as bad as a knockout or a referee stopped fight decision on a boxer's record).

News of the outstanding boxer travelled quickly and by 1914 he was engaged at the headquarters of boxing, The National Sporting Club in London. Jerry's London appearance was most impressive and in a completely one-sided fight he easily disposed of Brighton's

Danny Hughes. A month before the Hughes fight, Jerry had made an appearance at Birmingham when he outclassed 'Brummie' fighter Jack Ward, flooring him several times before a tenth round knock out. The Bradford lad had so won over the Midland's fans that the Birmingham promoter had no hesitation in booking Jerry again, this time against his best opponent to date, Willie Farrell. The match was fixed for £100 a side plus purse and at 9st 9lbs or under. Whilst Jerry had no problems making the weight, Farrell weighed in at 10st 3lbs and was extremely annoyed at having to forfeit £75 for being over the fixed weight. The legendary Jim Driscoll, through his friendship with Jerry's older brother Fred, was now taking an interest in the younger Delaney and 'Old Peerless' had no hesitation in telling his man to take the fight and ignore the weight advantage. Despite the forfeit, Farrell's backers were confident of making 'a bob or two' from the fight, but what a shock for them and what a disappointment for the packed house when the fight was all over inside two rounds. Delaney's accurate hitting had Farrell down in the first round, and three times in the second before the referee had no alternative but to stop it because Farrell was unable to defend himself. Farrell immediately clamoured

Willie Farrell who fought Jerry Delaney.

for a return claiming he was not fit for the fight and stating he was overweight because he was unable to train due to an ankle injury.

During the same period Jerry made, what was for him, a rare appearance in Yorkshire by fighting twice in Carlton Hill Barracks in Leeds. In the first one against George Ruddick of Leeds fixed for £180 a sidestake and purse. Jerry had so outclassed his man that by the third round it was a foregone conclusion as a result but surprisingly the referee prolonged it to round six when the towel was

Fred Welsh. The World Champion who opted to stay in America rather than fight Jerry Delaney.

thrown in. Nine year old Fred (the official Fred) Delaney was at the ringside for Jerry's second Leeds appearance. Going to Leeds for a youngster before the First World War was like going to London. Fred struggled to remember the fight in later life, but what did stand out in memory was on that day Jerry had beaten a Frenchman. Back street youngsters in 1913 had never seen 'a Frenchie' so Young Fred always had a crowd round when he related the tale of 'how our Jerry gave the Frenchman a good hiding'. Fernard Quendreux was not in the same class and was well beaten by the time the contest ended in the sixth round.

Jerry's latest round of success brought another engagement at the National Sporting Club. The matchmaker at boxing's headquarters was looking for an opponent to face the American Harry Stone. Newly arrived in this country the New Yorker had a reputation as one of the best lightweights in America. (Previous to his England visit Stone had beaten the best in Australia, including top British fighters John Summers, whom he beat twice, and Matt Wells who were both touring there). Still unbeaten Jerry was chosen as the man to try and put this cocky and extrovert American in his place. At the weigh-in before the fight, Stone smoking a huge black cigar of overpowering strength tried to make the ceremony a mockery by saying it was hardly worth bothering to put the gloves on for the punch it needed to beat his opponent. He even went as far as to ask Jerry whether he would not rather call the fight off and so save himself 'the father and mother of a hiding'. When the American loudmouth had left the smokefilled scaleroom leaving a parade of choking and eye watering onlookers, one wondered if the matchmaker had given young Jerry too daunting a task. The crowd was still apprehensive when Stone entered the ring smoking another of his horrible cigars, wearing a cloth cap and a dressing gown of many vivid colours. Trying not to look overawed Jerry knew the American would not have lasted two minutes with a partisan crowd back home, his brash attitude would have had the local clan baying for blood. The National Sporting Club were more refined, but they were shown to be a bit more boisterous than usual when Stone rushed at Jerry with bull at a gate tactics to try and justify his early predictions. When Delaney coolly sidestepped him and clipped his rival with a sting as he went floundering past, the crowd was right behind the Yorkshireman. Jerry than proceeded to give the American a boxing lesson and outclassed and outboxed him in every round. Stone changed his tactics at various stages of the fight, but he was no match for young Delaney who withstood his every manoeuvre. Realising he had little to fear from Stone, Delaney brought the crowd to their feet with a show of straight lefts, hooks, jabs and right uppercuts and it was only remarkable gameness that enabled Stone to be on his feet at the finish. Stone knew that he had been beaten by a better man and swallowed his pride to be the first to give the victor hearty congratulations. (Stone was around for a while. Llew Edwards the British and British Empire featherweight champion from 1915-17 had six clashes with him. Llew lost only thirteen in an over 100 fight career and four of them were against Stone and the American went twenty rounds with Ted Kid Lewis, the World welterweight champion in New Orleans).

In the euphoria of Jerry's great win, the acknowledged experts were tipping a great future for the Bradford lad and already comparisons were being drawn with Jim Driscoll and the World Champion Welshman Freddie Welsh (real name Freddie Thomas). Freddie had recently won the world title from American Willie Ritchie in London and immediately a suggestion was made that he should give Jerry a chance at his title. Welsh was said to be willing to fight Delaney for the title but he wanted a little breathing space first. The Welshman had been a spectator at the Stone fight and though he made a promise to fight Jerry in six months, maybe he realised Jerry was a real threat for he soon 'took his hook' over to America to look for more lucrative offers from American promoters.

The Somme - The Final Round
Within a fortnight of the Stone fight, the Great War had started. Jerry, as indeed many other British boxers, volunteered immediately for active service. Being in reach of a World title fight was put second to patriotism and Jerry enlisted in the Sportsman's Battalion. Brothers Jack, Frank and Joe also joined to serve, with the Delaney father proudly adding his name later.

Whilst in training prior to shipment to France there was time for two more contests in London. Following in the wake of Harry Stone came another American with the show business trimmings. Claiming an overwhelming record, Jack Denny strutted into London with the proclamation that he wanted to meet the best we could offer. With the Stone fight still fresh in memory, the National Sporting Club matchmakers looked no farther. Jerry was able to obtain the necessary leave and the punters had another boxing feast in store. It was another classic performance from the Broomfield idol. Denny had been expected to give Delaney a run for his money but only by consistent covering did the American manage to survive until the fourteenth round, when his seconds threw in the sponge. Denny had certainly met the best the country could offer. He was so outboxed that he never laid an effective punch for the whole fight. Two months later Delaney fought at the famous club in Covent Garden for the last time. Time was running out for the draft to France and Jerry used up leave time in which he could have journeyed home to give Willie Farrell another chance. Since the debacle of their first fight, Farrell had sought to wipe the slate clean. Willie had always stuck to the tale that he had been unlucky in their first meeting and with Jerry already the Sporting Club's firm favourite there was no problem in guaranteeing another full turn out for the return. To give Farrell his due he was worth another chance and the Bradford soldier's opponent put up a great performance in going the full twenty rounds. What was on show was another masterful performance from Jerry Delaney. Every technique was there for the crowd's approval. Close punching, long range jabbing, footwork and feints that made the audience purr with delight were paraded to such a degree of expertise, that despite Willie putting up the fight of his career, Jerry was a comfortable points winner. The stalwarts of the National Sporting Club eager for Jerry to be matched with Welsh cabled the Welshman in America warning him unless he defended his title against the official challenger, the lightweight crown would be declared vacant and Delaney would be given the first right to fight for it.

Jerry knew he was due to go abroad on the next draft. When there was talk of officials interposing on his behalf so that he could stay at home waiting the champions return, the Bradfordian decided his duties were with the lads on the front line. There was just time to squeeze in one more fight, when Jerry met Jack Greenstock at Liverpool in May 1915. Unfortunately it was not another classic. The fight produced little boxing due to the persistent holding and clinging of his opponent. Eventually by the seventh round the referee had had enough of these tactics and Greenstock was disqualified. No one was to know that Jerry had made his last appearance in the ring and as Jerry went over on the next draft, his proud record stood at thirty-five fights unbeaten (four of his thirty-five fights were draws. The Bobby Scanlon fight in New York was no contest, whilst J Robinson, Joby Jordan and Nat Williams got draw verdicts against him). Jerry went on the next draft as planned and was soon in the front line. After a few months of trench warfare, Lance Corporal Jerry Delaney was awarded the Distinguished Conduct Medal. After spending days cooped up in dug outs, Jerry and his squad mates were part of a dawn raid party over 'No Mans Land'. Laden with Mills bombs the plan was to drive the Germans back into their reserve trenches. The party had hardly moved out of their starting blocks, when a hail of bullets began to cut them down. Star shells illuminating the sky made the soldiers easy targets and the continuation of the mission foolhardy. With men dropping like nine pins the command was reluctantly to retreat. Running for his life Jerry copped for a bullet in the leg and another ripped through his sleeve. As he struggled back the boxing soldier noticed a fellow colleague, one who had befriended him before 'going over the top'. Ignoring his injuries, Jerry carried the unconscious soldier over his shoulder back to the lines. For the action Jerry was awarded his DSO. His gallantry award was well received back in Bradford. The concern over his injuries turned to relief when it was learned that his boxing career would not be curtailed and the great fighter could still nurse his unfulfilled ambition.

When they heard about his injuries, the city's boxing entrepreneurs Messrs Holloway, Coyle (still active in the sport since his early association with Paddy Mahoney), Embleton and Landlord of the Brownroyd Hotel Jack Midgley put on a benefit at the Palace for Jerry. Old rival Fred Blakeborough, a Lance Corporal in the 20th West Yorkshire left his instructor duties at Catterick to come and take part in an exhibition with Kid Eastwood. The occasion was highlighted by the appearance of the 'boy wonder' Alfie Hebblethwaite. (Poor Alfie, in the not too distant future, they would be having a benefit for him. Not a War victim because Alfie was too young for that, but a victim of unscrupulous promoters, who had burned him out after well over a century of ring fights whilst still in his teens).

After attention to his leg Jerry refused a physical training instructor position which would have guaranteed him a journey back to England and the prospects of more fights. Back in 'Blighty' he was a boxing hero, but in the trenches he was a soldier who wanted no differential treatment from the rest of the boys on the front line. Just over six months after his decoration, Jerry was one of the volunteers in a bombing raid at Delville Wood on the Somme. Fate decided he had answered his last bell as he was cut down in 'No Mans Land'.

British boxing still reeling after losing middleweight champion Tom McCormick only a few weeks previously, paid Jerry the honour at a tribute in *Boxing* (paper) by likening him to Sir Arthur Conan Doyle's legendary hero 'Champion Harrison', the man who had never won the big title but who nevertheless was so known and styled by his fellow ring heroes.

Although he was buried in France he was not forgotten, Lord Lonsdale headed a subscription, which reached a few hundred pounds, and a memorial was built in Bowling Cemetery.

Sports writers talk of star quality. Well one thing is for certain, Jerry was in that bracket and it is fitting that Bradford's greatest boxer has deservedly become a legend in sporting circles in his own town and that his name is not far from anyone's lips when some of the old timers reminisce on Bradford boxing.

CHAPTER 6

Prominent Bradford Boxers
Prior to the First World War

Tommy Cullen

Tommy Cullen was Bradford's most prominent boxer of the post Brassey era (1840) to the Paddy Mahoney era (1890). Affectionately known among the boxing fraternity as 'Old Peg Tops', Tommy Cullen fought in both the fist and glove periods.

Born in Ireland in 1850, he came to Bradford at an early age. After becoming interested in fighting after reading an article on self-defence he became a pupil of Tommy Williamson, the well-known trainer. After a spell with Johnnie Emmett he finished his apprenticeship under the wing of Tommy Kelly who had achieved his fistic fame by taking part in two great battles with Jack Rooke of Birmingham, winning one and losing the other. Cullen's first fight for money was against Tom Price of Brick Row (later Southgate). It was considered a cast iron certainty that Price would be the winner but the Irish man upset all the odds to take the verdict. Another hard fight followed, then came a great battle with the 'raw uns' against Jack Barber which lasted seventy-five minutes before Barber's seconds cried enough. His next fight, against A Johnson, was for £10, a huge sum for a local prizefight at that time. A story goes that a Bradford publican on showing what chances he thought 'Old Peg Tops' had, had edged a £5 note through from the corner, although there was no need as the contest proved Johnson had not an earthly.

Sponsored by a Bradford Alderman and a well-known local volunteer captain, Tom fought a memorable battle against Paddy Duffy of Birmingham at Doncaster Race Course when amidst tremendous rejoicing he had his best win to date. Tommy's crowning triumph came at Aldershot where a large boxing review was held with competitions at all weights. Cullen entered the nine stone class and went right through to win the championship. He was matched afterwards with Fahey of Leeds but the fight never came off. His career suddenly came to an end when he fell off a scaffold whilst engaged in his ordinary work. Although he had to spend the rest of his life in a wheelchair he still kept in touch with the local boxing scene and his son later ran promotions and became a top class judge.

Seth Rouse

Bradford's all round sportsman in the 1890s was Seth Rouse who took part in hundreds of money matches at various sports including swimming, arrow throwing, running, throwing the cricket ball and boxing. His running ability was well known and he was practically undefeated. At swimming he won matches for as much as £25 a side, a famous win being against Billy Underwood at Ripley Baths. In his time he swam at the Bill Haley Dam in Harold Park and the Cold Dam at Low Moor. His strength at throwing was second to none, arrow throwing being his specialty. Arrow throwing won him several £100 a side matches and a championship at Halifax Race course in 1886. Challenge matches for throwing the cricket ball were a regularity at the Old Red Gin fields and at Greenfield where the big crowds flocked when it was known Rouse was in action. He was a more than useful boxer and his record contained wins over George Dunn at the skating rink in four rounds, Jumper Smith at the Star Music Hall and Harry Robertshaw at the Jollity. Seth drew with Jonty Simpson at Carlisle Road Carpet Beating Room but lost to Elland's Jack Lamb at Trafalgar Street and to a character called 'Ponga' at the unlikely venue of 'Old Tom Cribbs Cabin'.

Dick Burge

Dick Burge moved to Bradford in 1894 to convalesce. Burge, who was from Newcastle, was one of the most prominent boxers in the country. Almost every day there was newspaper speculation of his comeback into the ring and talk of a fight against Jack Dempsey, the former middleweight champion, who was reputed to be coming to Britain with Jim Corbett. A three day benefit was held for his honour at the Grand Assembly Rooms at Briggate, Leeds, featuring Burge himself, Chesterfield Goole from London, Harry Thompson of Leeds, Bill Hatcher of London and the Denny Brothers from Australia. Burge did make a comeback and then retired for a while. By 1896 he was in a contest at the National Sporting Club against Kid Lavinge for the world lightweight championship which he lost by a knockout in the thirteenth round.

Fred Blakebrough.

Fred Blakeborough

One of the most popular boxers in Bradford's boxing history and ranking along with the two Delaney brothers as a top rated fighter in the years previous to and after the War was Fred Blakeborough. His first big impact fight was against Curly Osborne for £50 at the New Bradford Sporting Club at Thornbury. Osborne was a winner of over 200 fights, but not to be overawed Fred, who was barely seventeen, surprisingly took the verdict and during the same year he had verdicts over Tommy Curran at Liverpool and the return in Dublin.

A successful period at the beginning of 1913 when he beat Kid Vinton at Newcastle, Young Greenstock at Dublin and G Werner of London at Warrington inside a month brought him to the notice of A F Bettinson, the manager of the National Sporting Club. Bettinson fulfilled a promise he made to Fred when the youngster made his debut at boxing's headquarters in May. Losing a points verdict to Con Houghton the ex-amateur featherweight champion, he put up a good enough show to prove he was worthy of the occasion. Fred became a favourite at the Free Trade Hall, Manchester and in several appearances at the venue during 1914 he beat Harold Walker, proving beyond doubt that another win against a highly rated fighter from the Manchester area, Billy Marchant, was no fluke. A win against Teddy McGuiness when he was badly handicapped by a damaged eye, and a victory over Mick Gordon at St Helens put Fred's name forward as a contender to fight the champion Ted Kid Lewis. He was, in fact, due to fight Lewis in a non-title fight at the Olympia Skating Rink at Leeds in January 1914 when the fight was postponed due to a series of strikes in the town. In an eliminator held at the National Sporting Club with the winner due to fight for Lewis's title,

Fred was beaten by Seaman Hayes. Fred had built up a big lead in the fight only to lose by a chance blow in the later stages.

The intervention of the war saw Fred become an Army gymnasium instructor based at Catterick, and during his service he became a lightweight champion of all command home forces. His next fight after the Hayes fight saw Fred go through a rather sticky patch. He fought Joe Starmer of Kent at the Roundhay Rink, Leeds and adopted tactics which were very unusual for him, In a complete change of style he tried a rougher, more aggressive type of approach and the referee had to take the most unusual step of warning him several times. Forsaking his usual methods of completely outboxing his opponent and settling for hard won points victories to a style of trying to mix it led him to fall for a sucker punch twice in a fortnight.

Stationed at Catterick he was able to take a couple of bouts in the Northeast where among other matches he was beaten twice by Londoner George Groves. Despite his inconsistent form during this period he was given another chance at the National Sporting Club where in another eliminator, the winner to meet Duke Lynch for the championship, Fred met Welshman Llew Edwards. It was soon obvious Edwards was in a different class and despite a brave, spirited show by the Yorkshireman Jerry Delaney, Fred's second, had no choice but to throw the towel in after Fred had gone down twice in the tenth round.

Making a re-appearance after the war on Edwin Holloway's bill at Grimsby in 1919, Fred gave one of his best performances to beat Billy Benyon from Wales, the former British champion and Lonsdale Belt holder. Fred announced that while he was in the Army, he had been unable to confine himself to the lightweight division and intended making strides in the featherweight ranks. His next big fight was scheduled at Manchester against Francis Rossi for a purse of £250. Rossi's non-appearance and Fred's feeble performance against a much lighter substitute did little to enhance his championship hopes.

During 1921 after Edwin Holloway had decided to spend some time with other interests, Fred tried to keep the sport alive in his own time dabbling at promoting tournaments himself. Although he was still fighting during this period the realisation the following year that his best days had probably gone made him decide to hang up his gloves. Fred later became a star referee and a steward of the British Boxing Board of Control. Unfortunately he achieved fame through a couple of controversial decisions. In 1949 at Liverpool Stadium he disqualified local favourite Jimmy Molloy for a low punch and was threatened by angry spectators and in a return to Liverpool at a later period he put up the arm of the wrong man. Officiating in a bout featuring Pat McAteer, the British and British Empire middleweight, Fred put up the hand of McAteer's opponent Bill Ellaway. McAteer, it was reported, openly cried before Fred defused the situation and the riot that had broken out by stating 'Other people had come into the ring and my view was obscured, I thought I was holding up McAteer's arm.' He achieved national headlines over the Dave Charnley v Guy Garcia clash at Wembley. His points award to the Frenchman Garcia brought uproar. The British Lightweight champion, Charnley and his supporters stated they were making the strongest claims to the Board, even talking of taking court action to get the decision overturned. In fairness to Fred even the papers were undecided. Peter Wilson of the *Daily Mirror* gave Charnley seven out of ten rounds, Desmond Hackett of the *Daily Express* gave him six rounds, but Gerard Walter of the *News Chronicle* thought Garcia had just edged it.

In the latter years before he died in 1968 aged 74, Fred served his city in another way, he was a councillor for Bradford Moor from 1954-1959 and was president of Bradford Moor Conservative Club from 1958-1962.

Will Blakeborough
Perhaps overshadowed by Fred, the other Blakeborough brother Will had quite a small but successful career in the sport. Having the same problem as the Delaney's and his brother Fred during the period of non-activity due to the 1912-1914 ban on professional boxing in the city, Will moved up to the Northeast. Among his victories in 'Geordie Land' where decisions over Bill Cowley of Stockton, a points win over Jimmy Graves and a win over Billy Deane the Irish Bantam Champion. In his fight with Sheffield's Joby Jordan who had held Jerry Delaney to a draw, the referee had to intervene when Jordan had been sent to the canvas about six times. During 1914 Will fought in France (in fact the same night George Mitchell fought Carpentier), and despite a cut eye was a winner over six rounds against Frenchman Clement. Sadly Will's name was added to the list of killed in action whilst serving with the Bradford Pals in 1915 aged only twenty-two.

George Mitchell
George was an ex public schoolboy and son of a local mill owner, Tom Mitchell at Bingley, and though he was not really a boxer at all the one notable fight he had made his name known all over the country. His first love was wrestling and he became known locally in

Will Blakeborough with father Ben.

that sport as an amateur. He only turned to boxing as a bit of a
challenge when he entered the NCABA championships in Bradford
and surprisingly won the heavyweight class with ease.

Always on the look out for a bit of sport it was suggested as a joke
to have a bout with Georges Carpentier the famous boxer who was
being talked about all over the world. (Carpentier became the

scourge of British heavyweights and beat Joe Beckett, Bombardier Billy Wells and Ted Kid Lewis all in a round. He became light heavyweight champion of the World and fought Jack Dempsey for the World title). So money being no object, Mitchell and his friends went across to France to arrange the fight. George intended the fight to be secret but it leaked out and the 'mad Englishman' was the talk of France. Of course he stood no chance with Carpentier but he was hoping to last longer than the English heavyweight champion Wells who had been knocked out in just over a minute and it is rumoured he backed himself heavily to do so.

The fight which took place in April 1914 as expected was over in the first round with the result that George took a tremendous hiding but proving he had the pluck, if not the ability, to meet one of the best fighters in the world. Despite the fact of having to pay Carpentier £200 to enjoy being knocked out by him, the Yorkshire lad had the satisfaction of lasting a few seconds longer than Wells, and that was all he had hoped to do. There is a story that used to circulate telling about the time George and his father rumbled a burglar in their house. After he had been caught George's father propositioned the culprit with the choice of the police or a fight with George. No doubt the burglar was wise for he quickly chose the police. Rather sadly George was killed in action during the war whilst serving for the public school battalion in 1915, still in the youth of his life.

CHAPTER 7

The Pre-War Boxing Boom and the Ban on Professional Boxing in Bradford 1912-1914

B y 1910 the world boxing boom had arrived. The sport had become immensely strong in America, Australia and France, while in England the same interest had started to develop. In London by 1911, five new boxing halls, all capable of holding between 7,000 and 10,000 had opened. In Bradford it saw the beginnings of contests at Belle Vue Barracks and the Central Baths Hall. Especially noticeable was the Army's interest in this sport. Encouragement was given among its ranks to any budding fighters and training was available to teach any raw recruits the rudiments of the sport. The Army helped further popularise the sport by promoting and making readily available venues like the drill halls at Leeds, Halifax, Bingley, Keighley and the Belle Vue Barracks on Manningham Lane.

The main man responsible for the interest in boxing was the new World heavyweight champion Jack Johnson. The fact that he was coloured and the fact that he ostentatiously acted the part made him a hate target. Competitions were set up all over the world to find a boxer capable of beating 'that brash nigger'. Crowds had flocked to the St George's Hall to see the New Century Pictures film of Johnson's victory over Tommy Burns. (The former Canadian World Champion Burns once took part in a famous fight in Leeds, although very few of the public saw it, the action scene was a city hotel. Burns had visited England in 1908 prior to sailing to Australia with Johnson on his heels. Twelve years later he returned at the age of 39 partly to inspect the current British 'white hopes'. Convinced he could beat our best man he went into strict training and issued a challenge to British champion Joe Beckett. There was a thirteen-year age gap when Burns stepped into the Royal Albert Hall ring and it was soon obvious that the gap was too wide. By the seventh round Beckett had shut the Canadian up and restored British pride. The sequel to the fight took place a few months later when Burns severely criticised Beckett's performance against Frank Moran. Not long after the fight both boxers, along with quite a few others, were invited to take part in a charity performance for ex-servicemen at Leeds. The best scrap of the evening wasn't at the venue, but at the hotel where both parties were staying. After both men had met on the hotel steps a heated disagreement took place resulting in a real set to and it was generally agreed by onlooking boxers who eventually stopped it, that Burns had certainly squared matters with the British champion).

During December 1911, Johnson was booked for a week's engagement at the Palace Theatre. His proposed visit created great interest amongst the public in Bradford and during the days prior to his engagement the controversial character was built up as a giant of all proportions. Large crowds gathered in the railway station anticipating his arrival. Much to the crowd's disappointment it was learned that Johnson was unable to fill the booking through illness. The cancellation was a double upset for the Palace proprietors had guaranteed full houses for the duration of his visit.

Boxing's new found popularity was not approved of in every quarter, the Home Secretary made a decision to stop Johnson's proposed fights with the British Champion Bombardier Billy Wells in 1911. He was supported by a petition from the Rev Roberts and signed by the Lord Mayor and some of the members of the Bradford City Council. The three main reasons for stopping the fight were -

1. Because such a contest would be unavoidably brutal and degrading and cannot in any way be called friendly.
2. Such a contest between black and white may endanger the friendly relations between the two races.
3. Because the reproduction of the fight in picture shows is being organised in a large scale and will definitely extend its baneful influence.

The chief constable of Bradford, Mr Farndale, made an announcement early in 1912 that no licences would be given to allow professional boxing in the city. He stated that he did not wish to stop boxing, but they would have to be exhibition only and not decided by a knock out blow. He stopped Fred Delaney training in a public house and also substituted wrestling for boxing in the Bradford City Police Club. The embargo lasted over two years and although the boxing boom in that period continued, Bradford had no part in it.

It was a poor state of affairs for the boxing fan who had to travel to Leeds or other towns to see the sport, especially in a prolific period in Bradford boxing where the town in the Delaney brothers, Jerry and Fred, and Fred Blakeborough who were fighting out of other areas like the Northeast, had three boxers in the frame to fight for championship honours. It was rather co-incidental that when the Chief Constable relented and gave permission for a professional contest to be held at Belle Vue Barracks on 28 May 1914, it was announced a couple of weeks previously that the King was a boxing fan and several champions would be appearing in his honour.

CHAPTER 8

Joe Fox

Coming to prominence in the years before the First World War, for over half a century bantam and later featherweight champion, Joe Fox was the only Leeds born boxer to win a British championship.

Born in February 1892 Joe was a member of a famous boxing family that lived in Benson Street, off North Street. His three brothers all became involved in the sport. George was a good boxer who emigrated to Australia in the mid twenties. Benny was well known as a manager and Percy who travelled and went to America (as Joe did later to fight) and became a promoter in the sport and a bookmaker.

Joe's career started in 1909 when he took his early fighting steps in the fairground booths. Soon achieving notoriety Joe was picked up by a member of another famous Leeds boxing family Jack Green and by 1910 young Fox started appearing at local venues. In 1911 at the Sporting Club Thornbury, Joe suffered an early setback when the much more experienced 'Sticker' Will Atkinson from Bradford proved too good for the youngster. Eager to learn from his defeat the ever improving Fox met Sticker again a few months later at Carlton Hill barracks and avenged the defeat by completely out-boxing his opponent. Joe had three classic encounters with another Bradford boxer, Fred Blakeborough. The first two were draws while the third meeting ended with Blakeborough being disqualified. Another young fighter Joe met three times in 1912 was flyweight Bill Ladbury. Joe lost the first two encounters but knocked Ladbury out in five rounds in the pair's third fight. The following year Ladbury became British and World flyweight champion but was tragically killed in action in 1917.

In 1914 Joe Fox followed the trend and went to America with a stable of English fighters, which included Frank Moody and Bermondsey Billy Wells. Fights in America during that period were classed as no decision contests on records. The usual format being that the reporting newspaper gave unofficial verdicts in its coverage.

Joe Fox. Leeds double chamption at the early twenties.

In his first tour the only boxer to really beat the Leeds man was Eddie Campi in Boston. Campi being a claimant to the World bantam title having beaten the great Frenchman Charles Ledoux in 1912. Among his paper wins were verdicts over Dutch Brant, Peter Herman (World bantam champ three years later) and Tommy O'Neill.

Back home under the managership of Harry Dorsey and the man with the reputation as the best trainer in England, Jack Goodwin, Joe continued his form which had already come under the notice of the National Sporting Club's manager 'Peggy' Bettinson. After appearances at 'boxing headquarters', Joe was matched in an eliminator for the bantam title with Scot Alex Lafferty. Joe beat Lafferty over eighteen rounds and he expected to fight the champion Curly Walker, but Walker had weight trouble and when he had to relinquish the title, Fox was matched with tough Newcastle miner Jimmy Berry for the vacant title at the National Sporting Club.

On 22 November 1915, the Yorkshireman became British bantam champion. His straight left and speedier approach were too much for Berry for whom his seconds threw in the towel during the eighteenth round. The fight was quickly followed by a quick defence against Tommy Harrison 'The Pride of the Potteries'. After completing another victory came the chance of winning a Lonsdale Belt outright against Joe

Symmonds from Plymouth who had been the flyweight champion until the immortal Jimmy Wilde beat him. Betting was close for a fight worth £375 (included purse and side bets). Living up to his name of Fox, the Leeds man with the rare talent of making his opponent fight the way he wanted them to fight was too crafty and speedy for the challenger. Symmonds tired in the later stages and the fight was over in the eighteenth round and Joe Fox became the outright owner of a Londsale Belt.

During 1916 Fox made two appearances in Bradford against two former British bantam champions. The Windsor Baths were sold out for weeks at both promotions to see the local champion in action. In the first fight he beat Welshman Billy Benyon while the second proved a revenge match against Digger Stanley who, a year previously, had beaten Fox in a non-title fight. (Legend had it that Digger – real name George – who was born in Norwich and at the time of his fight with Fox was fighting out of Liverpool, was the son of a Gypsy and was sold for a sovereign and a pint of beer. Reared in the boxing booths it was always thought he was about ten years older than the age he quoted). The return was a superb clash, which unfortunately exploded in the tenth round when Stanley who was always talked about as the best fighter to appear at the National Sporting Club was disqualified for butting.

The call of America again in 1918 saw Joe give up his British title to make another stateside trip. The Leeds boxer was now operating as a featherweight and as the world champion was an American; his thoughts were of a tilt at the champion. Boxing was still being frowned upon in some of the states and bouts were still taking place on an exhibition basis. Joe met the champion in question, Johnny Kilbane in a six round match in Philadelphia and gave a good account of himself against a man rated the best in the world. On the same trip he had no-decision contests against Eddie Campi whom he had met on his first American trip and Joe Lynch the future World bantam champion.

Back in England Joe made his first appearance as a featherweight in England against Salford's Billy Marchant at Windsor Baths, Bradford. Marchant had recently lost to Mike Honeyman in a fight for the vacant British featherweight title. The fight, one of the highest purses in Bradford was for £200 a side and a promoter's purse of £500. By the third round the fight was over in dramatic fashion. Marchant rushed Fox and the latter ducked and in doing so got his head between the Salford man's legs and lifted him onto his shoulders. The Leeds boxer shook him off and dropped the dazed

Marchant with a short right to the chin. The incident happened as the bell sounded and as Marchant was unable to come out for the next round Fox was the winner.

In October 1921, Joe who had never lost a bantam title fight got his chance to fight for the British title against Mike Honeyman, who since his defeat of Tancy Lee was going for his third outright win. Although the fight didn't turn out to be a classic Joe did enough to take the verdict and receive the honour of becoming a double champion.

During May 1922 at Holland Park Skating Rink in a National Sporting Club promotion, Joe was matched against Frenchman Eugene Criqui. The match was billed as for the European title and an eliminator for the World title. The title was actually in dispute because the European crown was also being claimed by Billy Matthews who earlier had won the title beating the Belgian holder Arthur Wyns but because he wasn't a British champion the National Sporting Club decided he had no official right to have fought for the title in the first place. So confident was the Leeds camp that Fox's backer, Leeds bookie Dave Goodman, offered a £500 side bet on the result plus a racehorse for Fox if he won. It seemed as if all Leeds were having a bob or two on their hero for Joe Fox's reputation as a winner of money matches was second to none. He might lose an occasional overweight match but the canny Jew never lost at 8st 6lb with the incomparable Jack Goodwin as his trainer. Fox made all the running his flying fists making the French Bantam champion look like a tenth rater, and with the way Joe was outboxing Criqui, Fox's Leeds fans in the audience were rubbing their hands with anticipation. Before the fight the Frenchman had received a cable from Paris to say his wife was seriously ill and Criqui's manager had a real task to persuade him to fight. Criqui's efforts were futile and it was obvious that his thoughts were elsewhere and with a home win looking certain, already the victory smile had broadened Joe's lips. Events turned dramatically in the twelfth. Criqui's manager the famous Descamps seeing the situation was hopeless as his boxer was far too behind on points, prompted him to make a do or die effort in the twelfth round which paid dividends. The Frenchman pulled out a left hook followed by a hard right early in the round and the tide turned very quickly. Down again in the next round the referee stopped it when Fox looked to be taking a breather. As the referee pointed to Criqui as the winner the crowd roared its disapproval. Despite protests he stuck to his decision. Later in the year Criqui beat Matthews and went to

America and in June 1923 the man with the iron jaw (this name originating from the time a First World War bullet had smashed his jaw. It was patched with wire and plaster and as a result it was said he couldn't be knocked out) beat Kilbane for the World title. Kilbane, due to circumstances in America had been world featherweight champion for eleven years, longer than anyone else in the division had.

Disappointed, Joe relinquished his British title and with the proud record of never being beaten in a British title fight set sail for a World tour taking in America and Australia. On his return in 1925, Joe challenged the new featherweight champion Johnny Curley of Bermondsey. As the National Sporting Club was not in session two London promoters secured the match for Brighton, which was at the height of its holiday season. Two nights prior to the fight two local gangs had fallen foul of one another in a Brighton club. The club was smashed up and there was damage at the Pavilion after the two rival groups had moved on. The boxing match had cornered the Brighton betting fraternity and trouble was nailed on when the two gangs bet on different boxers. When the balloon went up when fighting broke out in the crowd it very quickly spread to a full-scale battle. Undeterred the two men carried on fighting and with a big crowd round the referee baying for blood and blood and guts on the floor and the referee's old glasses lying on the floor broken, he decided to play safe and give the fight verdict a draw.

There were only a few fights left before Joe retired in 1926. One of his last fights was a win over another future Yorkshire double champion, Sheffield's Johnny Cuthbert (Johnny would take Curley's featherweight title) who stated he had learnt more in one fight than in all his previous bouts.

After retiring Joe settled down to marry and moved to Birmingham where he took a tobacconist's shop and spent the rest of his days.

CHAPTER 9

Tommy Rowan
Keighley's First Boxing Hero

The first boxer to make a name for himself from Keighley was Tommy Rowan. Born in 1883 Tommy got his early taste of pugilistic action when the visiting fairs appeared in the vicinity. His performances in the boxing booths where he fought with such notables as Iron Hague were enough encouragement for him at the unusually late age for a fighter of twenty-seven, to take up the sport seriously.

From 1910 to the commencement of the First World War the sixth battalion West Yorkshire regiment promoted boxing at the Drill Hall, and it was at this venue that Tommy first made a name for himself winning an open age 9st 7lb competition in one of the early promotions. This in itself was not a bad achievement as Tommy was about a stone less than the entrance weight. Working locally as a comb maker and training at the *Angel Inn*, Leeds Street, it was not long before a reputation was built up and he became a great favourite at Keighley Drill Hall.

A brilliant twelve round victory over Charlie McGowan for a £10 purse and £5 side stake in 1911 was his first important victory. It was especially pleasing to the Keighley fans as McGowan came to the town with a good record built up in Bradford. Tommy beat another Bradford man in this period, Don Leavy of Manningham knocking his man out inside the distance. He was matched three times against Arthur Wood and beat him on each occasion including once at the Keighley Hippodrome in Hanover Street.

In December 1913 at the Drill Hall, he fought his best opponent to date, Kid Kelly another Bradford fighter who had been a top boxer in the area for several years, and among his achievements was an Army championship in India in 1909. Fixed at fifteen rounds, and for what was a large purse and side stake in Keighley at £65, Tommy's performance was so superior that after three rounds Kelly was forced to retire due to an extremely badly cut eye. To be fair to Kelly he had

Tommy Rowan.

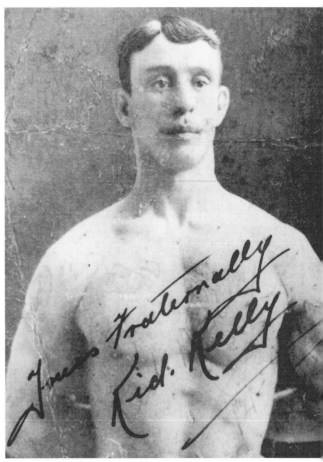

Manningham fighter **Kid Kelly** was Tommy's first big name victory.

taken the fight at a week's notice after a lengthy absence from the ring, even so it was thought he would have too much experience for Tommy. This win delighted the Keighley supporters and Tommy quickly became an idol in the town. There was a definite rivalry between Keighley and Bradford and the victory so excited the fans that a local wit wrote a poem in honour of the fight, advising that any other boxer from Bradford who dared to come and meet their champion would end up the same way.

The rivalry was extended to another match with a Bradford man in March 1914. Tommy's opponent this time was one of the bravest men to ever enter the ring. Sticker Atkinson whose career went back before the turn of the century when he had won a championship of the North contest at Bradford's St George's Hall and had in his time fought some of the best men in the country. Now at the back end of his career even though he was the same age as Tommy he was content to be a stumbling block to some of the area's aspiring champions. In this very role he had been the first man to beat Joe Fox, the winner of the British bantamweight title in 1915, although he had been beaten in the return. Sticker, the nickname derived from his courage as a non quitter in the ring, had taken part in some of the most brutal fights which had left the scars of a badly ulcerated stomach, the very condition which saw him invalided out of the Army. To say he should not have recommenced boxing was an understatement. But this was Sticker Atkinson the man who could not resist a challenge. Keighley Drill Hall was packed to the door with a sprinkling of Atkinson's supporters who had travelled through for the fight. The result was a great battle with Tommy taking the early honours, his quick firing punching closing Atkinson's eye. Despite the handicap Sticker stuck to his name and put up a very spirited show. Sheer determination had carried him through the fight and in the eyes of his supporters that was enough to take the decision. When the decision went to Tommy, much to the delight of the Keighlians, the ever controversial Sticker stated that the result was a hometown decision and made a declaration hat he could get the backing to fight Rowan anywhere but Keighley. Tommy was so incensed with Atkinson's behaviour that he offered the Bradford fighter out there and then round the back door. The War saw there was never a return and although there was further appearances from Tommy in the ring, Sticker's health finally got the better of him.

In 1916 Tommy took part in an experimental open-air tournament at Bradford City's ground at Valley Parade. In front of the biggest crowd he had fought, Tommy was matched with Kid Eastwood of Brighouse. Eastwood, winner of the Northern Area Featherweight title and much the younger man was the slight favourite as the men entered the ring. After putting up a creditable performance in the first half a dozen rounds, the turning point came in the seventh when a burst glove aggravated Tommy's eye, enabling Eastwood to do enough to make the referee stop the fight.

In July 1920 Keighley's discharged, demobbed soldiers and sailors organised boxing shows at Albert Street Baths and in the first show Tommy now in the veteran stage announced his final contest. The local favourite's appearance drew a capacity crowd and much to their delight Tommy beat his opponent Billy Austin in three rounds. The next performance at the Baths was a benefit match for Rowan in which many well-known boxers appeared including the Delaney Brothers.

The following year popular Bingley man, C Crook, took over promotions in Keighley and Harry Chester also from Bingley and an extremely promising young fighter was his regular top of the bill boxer. After Chester had beaten Austin Niland who boxed as Sapper George Clark, whom Tommy had been coaching, the Keighley boxing crowd persuaded Tommy to make a comeback and put this young Chester in his place. The fight aroused a great deal of interest and with the promoter putting up a £20 purse plus his backer's sidestakes, the baths was full to capacity. Tommy was now aged thirty-eight and was sadly no match for the younger man. Only a shadow of his former self, Tommy's end came after only eighty-five seconds. Tommy wasn't lost from boxing; he kept an interest in the local boxing scene and helped Johnny Barratt, a future Keighley boxing star.

CHAPTER 10

Harry Mason

One of the great characters in boxing between the two wars was Hebrew Harry Mason who, in a seventeen year career amassed over two hundred fights and after first becoming a champion as early as twenty had the rare distinction of winning two British titles twice.

Born in Whitechapel in London on 1903, Harry moved with his parents to Leeds as a youngster because London was considered too risky with the zeppelin air raids. After gaining his first boxing interest as a member of the Jewish Lads Brigade he was winning schoolboy competitions whilst still under six stone. After turning pro at seventeen it was not long before he was appearing on Sunday morning shows at Foster Thompson's gymnasium in Newcastle Street. It was obvious from his early victories at the Leeds 'threepenny shops' (derived from the fact that as these shows were held on a Sunday it was illegal to charge admission, so instead the organisers had a silver collection of which in those days threepence was the lowest coin) that he had something special and he was soon chalking up a run of local consecutive victories, being particularly popular at Fenton Street Barracks. After winning his three debut fights in 1920, his 1921 record ran fifteen wins from eighteen.

As Harry built up his name a similar reputation grew about his cockiness which he deliberately exaggerated every time he appeared in the ring. Reminiscent of the early days of Cassius Clay and the later Prince Naseem Hamed, crowds started to flock to see the irate Jewish boy knocked off his perch. Built on the small side but well proportioned, Mason had learnt his craft quickly and well and by the time he was twenty, he was the leading challenger for the British lightweight title held by Seaman Hall.

Seaman, who was managed by Ted Broadribb, knew that Mason was a tricky customer and knew all the tricks in the book and some that weren't in it! For a while Harry had gone under the name 'Little Fiddler', not because he was a violinist, but for the way he could easily make his opponent commit errors. A purse was accepted from

Harry Mason. the Leeds double champion. *Bill Matthews*

Harry Mason the fighter the fans loved to hate.

promoter Arnold White, and Mason met Hall for the British and European lightweight title at Olympia in May 1923. Six months earlier the pair had boxed a twenty round draw at London's Premierland. Referee Joe Palmer was in charge and he was later to reflect in print that Mason was the most elusive customer in the ring and one of the few who knew how to mill on the retreat. 'Nobby' Seaman Hall couldn't corner Harry who was too slippery and Mason's craftiness of darting in and out saw the challenger move ahead on points. Things exploded in the ninth round, when Hall dropped Harry. There was an immediate cry for foul by Mason's corner. When Palmer told Harry he was in danger of disqualification himself, Mason who had been ordered to stay down by his corner, eventually rose and Palmer, after admonishing Hall, told the two fighters to box on. Twice more Harry complained of low punches and after Seaman was cautioned in round twelve the action terminated in the next round. Mason was down again and this time Palmer disqualified the champion, and Harry Mason, the cocky Jew, the man the crowd loved to hate had won his first British title. Though not a title fight the pair met again five months later and after Harry beat the ex-champion far more convincingly, Hall's career at thirty-one was over as far as title stakes were concerned.

Previous holder, Ernie Rice, who had lost his title to Hall, was Harry's first challenger and the adopted Yorkshireman beat him over twenty rounds.

During the twenties it was fashionable for the best British fighters to try their luck in America. Harry went hoping to get a crack at the World Champion Benny Leonard. Although the Leonard fight did not take place, he distinguished himself losing three out of eight fights with most of his contests being against welterweights, for Harry had put on a few pounds on the boat going over. In his absence, the National Sporting Club deprived Harry of his title and a competition was held to find a new champion. Ernie Izzard the 'Hearne Hill Hairpin' beat Jack Kirk from Doncaster to claim the title. Harry, on hearing the news, had rushed back from the States and was forced to watch the competition to find his successor. Mason, naturally, was straight in with a challenge to the new champion and Harry Jacobs offered £750 for a championship match between the pair to take place at The Royal Albert Hall. Well aware of Mason's talents, Izzard elected to defend his title against Bermondsey boy Teddy Baker who was the official NSC challenger, even though the fight with Mason was worth considerably more. Izzard beat Baker on points and two months after that win he met Harry. The National Sporting Club aware of the interest in a clash with Mason arranged the fight at Holland Park and this time Harry had the chance to win a Lonsdale Belt. (His earlier title fights were not under the auspices of the NSC hence no belts were ever awarded. Izzard was now going for his third belt). Weeks before Mason had been fighting in London, when Izzard had entered the ring prior to the action and needled Harry by being announced as the British Champion. The incident upset Zalic Goodman, Harry's trainer, who socked Izzard whilst Mason was restrained. The incident and the known needle between the two claimants made sure Holland Park was over-spilling.

Mason started the fight with something to prove and unsettled Izzard with his non-stop attack. The champion found it hard to cope as Harry forged ahead in the early rounds. In the eighth Mason, with a left hook followed by a right cross, had Izzard down. The noise was so loud that after what he had judged was ten seconds Mason helped his opponent up from the canvas. The fight was in the days when the official was outside the ring and seeing the fight was not; in fact, over Harry launched into another round of blows. Once again Izzard went down all over the place and once again the fight was not over for the bell had sounded ending the round. The action had caused excitement between the two sets of fans in the audience and fists flew as the two groups tried to emulate their man. When he thought he had heard the gong the impatient Harry tried to get at Izzard but couldn't because he was surrounded by a bunch of seconds. The referee now decided to enter the ring and Harry was sent back to his corner. It was announced Izzard had been disqualified for being unable to continue and Mason was declared the champion. Though there was no real doubt that Izzard was finished, a riot nearly ensued and this fight above any other infuriated boxing fans against Mason. His big headedness meant he was booed and barracked every time he entered the ring. Forever pulling tricks on boxers and referees he was even disliked in Yorkshire. When he fought Jack 'Cast Iron' Casey at Heslops Stadium in East Street, he irritated the crowd further by throwing the gloves in the audience and demanding another pair.

Promoter Harry Jacobs always keen to get Mason in the ring, gave Harry the chance to become double champion when he matched the British lightweight champion against Scot, Hamilton Johnny Brown (the Hamilton before his name was to avoid confusion with Johnny Brown, the British bantam champion) for the British welterweight title. Brown had challenged Seaman Hall unsuccessfully for the lightweight title in 1923 and moving up to welterweight had lost to the great Ted Kid Lewis in a bid to win the welter crown the following year. Another Scot, Tommy Milligan, had ended Lewis's reign and as Milligan had gone to America to further his career, Jacobs considered the title vacant. (On his return Milligan moved up to middleweight and won the British title). Though normally the fans were against Mason they were on his side against the Scotsman at the Royal Albert Hall. Brown knew the task was hard against a fighter of Harry's calibre and he made sure he was as fit as he could be for the occasion. The result was controversial, Mason's supporters thought he had won and although Brown got full points for effort Mason seemed to make him miss more than he made contact and there was an uproar when Brown was announced the winner. The crowd eventually subsiding when Ted Kid entered the ring to raise Mason's hand as a gesture. There was obvious clamour for a return and Jacobs was delighted with a record attendance at the Royal Albert Hall when Brown and Mason met again the following month in November 1925. The second fight was close until Mason proved the stronger in the late rounds by putting the Scot down in the fifteenth round. Credit to Brown he came back in desperation to hold onto his title, but after a grandstand finish between the two boxers the referee, C H Douglas, gave Harry the nod and Brown's reign as champion was over after only forty-two days and Harry Mason was a double champion.

For his first fight in 1926 Mason was matched with Ernie Rice who was given another crack at the lightweight crown. The occasions brought another disqualification award, which saw Harry retain his title. Immediately after Harry decided to relinquish the smaller weight championship. To take the Rice fight he had to lose weight so it was easier staying in the welter range. Even though he had got to

Harry Mason (Leeds and Whitechapel).

the top the adopted Yorkshireman still continued to carry out his outrageous antics which had now become his trademark. He loved the show business side of the sport, always smartly dressed, his hair always immaculately oiled down with a middle parting and never at a loss for words. He liked his photo in the papers; he performed tap dancing on stage, was an expert ballroom dancer and skater and had taken to riding in Rotten Row. He formed and led a dance band, which once topped the bill at Holborn Empire. His style did not go down with everyone for once at Blackfriars, fans completely ruined his car outside. Despite his deliberate attempts to infuriate fans, there was no doubting his brilliant skills as a boxer. His ring craft combined with nimble footwork and defensive ability made him a joy to watch. Another referee to praise Mason to the hilt was Eugene Henderson who remarked 'Mason was the first man to make me realise the full difficulties of refereeing'. The international referee added: 'Harry was the most knowledgeable man I have ever had to control for he knew more about in-fighting than almost any other boxer'.

Two months after the Rice fight Harry was matched with the eighteen-year-old teenage sensation Len Harvey for his British welterweight title. Harvey had started as a thirteen-year-old in Plymouth boxing six, two-minute rounders and since his rise to a title challenger he had become a firm favourite at Blackfriars. Harvey had just ended a forty-two match undefeated run to Johnny Sullivan, a decision that referee, Joe Palmer, was heavily criticised for. Mason himself was only twenty-three but was a veteran of eighty-four fights and had already contested six title fights and tasted the American experience. The match with Len was a quick sell out at the Royal Albert Hall and Mason promised the youngster a boxing lesson. Harry had ballooned up to 11st 4lbs before the fight and had got himself fit under top trainer Alec Goodman. C H Douglas was in charge and there was a large contingent of Harvey's Blackfriars fans. The fight had a sensational opening when the crowd thought the challenger was going to win it in the first round. A right from the youngster put Mason down, but luckily for Harry the punch did not catch him fully and he was straight back up and quick to show he wasn't hurt. Mason went through his 'bag of tricks' but could not unsettle Harvey who was showing maturity beyond his years. A right clip brought Mason to his knees, but Harvey held off thinking the foxy champion might be kidding. Harry became stronger in the middle of the fight and looked to be taking a lead on points. Len put Harvey down again in the eighteenth round but Mason while thought to be hurt was able to work it off. Harvey's good start and finish made the onlookers think he had taken the verdict. Douglas decided he couldn't separate them and gave the verdict a draw. Mason retaining his title was not popular, a draw was a rare result and general opinion was that Harry had some of lady luck on his side. Harvey went on to become one of Britain's greatest boxers. Moving up to middleweight to win British and British Empire championships, he later took the two same titles at light heavy weight and heavyweight and in 1939 he won a version of the world light heavyweight title.

Harry met his match in May 1926 when Birmingham's Jack Hood took away his welterweight title to the joy of jubilant London supporters at Holland Park. A return was held a couple of months later and Hood showed he was Mason's master by repeating his points victory. Hood was to remain champion for eight years before he finally relinquished the welter title. (For five years he never defended the welter title and had three unsuccessful attempts at Harvey's middleweight crown).

Despite having no titles Harry never lost his popularity both in the capital and in the provinces. Defeats did start to figure more on his record. Lightweight champion Fred Webster proving a difficult opponent, Webster licking him three times out of their four meetings. After Hood had relinquished and not too long after retired, Mason was given the chance at thirty-one to win his welter title back when he was matched with 'Tiger' Len Smith at Birmingham in 1934. Harry regained his old title; it had been eleven years since he had first won a British title, when he won on one of the disqualification's that seemed to haunt his career, in the fourteenth round. Now a double champion twice, Harry's hold on his title didn't last the year out.

After his title reclamation, Harry did not fight for five months before meeting Midlands boxer, Pat Butler. Butler had beaten Len Wickwar in an unofficially arranged eliminator and it was assumed that if Butler won the twelve round match Harry would give the twenty-one year old Leicester man a crack at his title. Butler was managed by George Biddles who would climax a lifetime in boxing when his fighter, Richard Dunn, fought Muhammad Ali for the World title in 1976. As usual the over confident Mason started to pile up the points, but he had overestimated Butler who seeing Mason was in difficulties in the later rounds, the lay off from his sport had begun to affect Harry and spurred on by his hometown crowd put Harry down in the eleventh round. Butler's efforts to knock Harry out were spoiled by the youngster's overeagerness, which saw many wild punches miss. Harry agreed to defend against Butler, but he had demanded £800. Biddles, eager for his man not to miss out, took the title fight at Leicester's Granby Halls with no money guarantee and told the promoters to 'pay us what you can afford!' Mason was fitter than in his last fight but had trouble keeping the youngster at bay. After the first half a dozen rounds had proved even, Butler began to get on top as Harry began to tire. Harry surprised the crowd by having something in reserve and his skill seemed to threaten the hold Butler had gathered in the fight. The referee gave it to Butler, but the decision was controversial even some of Butler's supporters thought Mason would hold onto his title.

Though he was the new champion things did not turn out too well for the Leicester man. The promoter had lost £300 on the fight so Butler won nothing but the title and his career nose-dived so much that by 1936 he had retired without even defending his title. Harry's career lasted into 1937, he brought the curtain down on his illustrious eighteen year career at 140 wins from 208 contests when he lost to Ted Kid Berg the former world junior welterweight champion in his last ring appearance.

After the end of his ring career, Harry joined the RAF where he served thirteen years as physical instructor. Later Harry and his family moved to South Africa to take a hotel in Durban. When he revisited Leeds in the 1960s to look some old friends up and relive some great moments, he disclosed he had moved to Capetown where he was earning his living as a masseur and gym attendant.

Harry Mason passed away in 1977 and though he will go down as one of the country's great boxing characters, he was also one of the country's greatest ring tacticians.

CHAPTER 11

An Array of Leeds Bantams - Leeds Boxers Between the Wars

As well as Harry Mason and Joe Fox, Leeds was served with several class fighters in the years between the Wars. There was a luxury of good boxers in the smaller divisions with bantams in particular flying the Leeds flag.

Billy Shaw from the Foster Thompson stable and Kirkstall boy Alf Thornhill were rated flyweights whilst bantam Walter Stanton who was very active at local venues performed so well in exhibition with Jimmy Wilde that when Stanton made his next ring appearance, the champion Wilde turned up to referee. Billy Miller was tipped for championship honours in the bantam division aged only eighteen after beating Scottish champion Jim Mahorg in the Tommy Farr versus Eddie Pierce bill at the Olympic. Billed as the 'Northern Stylist' his career included defeats over several champions in the mould of Welshman Mog Mason, Romanian Jan Sandu, Scot Jim Knowles and the former British flyweight champion Bert Kirby.

Well remembered from the era were the clashes between those two great rivals Benny Thackray and Little Minor. As both men were leading contenders in the bantam division, it was obvious that a match between the pair would be a great attraction in the city. It was the classic battle. Thackray the stylist versus Minor the fighter. Fixed at a purse of £200, Harry Minor had to spend the afternoon prior to the fight at the Russian baths in Cookridge Street sweating off the surplus. Thackray was too good for Harry on the day and in two other meetings Thackray repeated the victory while Harry got his verdict on a foul.

Both men fought Johnny King the British and British Empire bantam champion, Benny going on to have six clashes with 'Kingie' and also two with the 'Manchester Express'. Jackie Brown, who was the Lancashire city's only World champion from 1933 to 1996. (Brown was the world flyweight champion from 1932 to 1935 before losing his title to Benny Lynch. He moved up to bantam to

Benny Thackray.

unsuccessfully challenge his stablemate King for the British Bantam title in 1937). Johnny King finished his 1930 stint off with points wins over two Leeds men at Roynton. Spike Bradley was beaten over twelve rounds after surviving four counts at various stages of the fight and little Minor who was sent to the floor by Kingie's right hand in round two recovered splendidly to lose a close fifteen round contest.

In March 1931, King met his third Leeds man when he was matched with Benny at Blackpool Tower. Benny had heard from Harry about King's much talked about right hand bomb and was experienced enough to keep well out of its range. Early in the fight King damaged his right hand and it affected the rest of the contest for he could only use it sparingly. Going into the last rounds the fight was so close. Johnny went for it, throwing caution to the wind and trying to catch Thackray with a series of wild right hands. The result was a draw and the general opinion was that King was fortunate. King requested a return and the two men met at Belle Vue five weeks later. Again Thackray proved too elusive; he never let King settle and the frustrated Mancunian lost a points decision. Benny had been too clever, but King's handlers knew he would learn from the two encounters. Indeed he did, for he never lost another fight until the end of the year when he made a failed attempt at the British bantam title against Dick Corbett. The run of victories included King's first win over Thackray at the third attempt when he stopped Benny in twelve rounds at Royton. In November 1931 Benny Thackray got his chance against Jackie Brown. The Manchester flyweight by then had won and lost the British flyweight title to Bert Kirby and had been European champion since May and had successfully defended it twice. Brown had only been married three weeks before the fight but it didn't affect him and Benny couldn't claim a double over the two great Manchester champions. Since 1928 Brown had only lost six times in 46 fights (Sheffield's Dixie Inkles held two decisions over him) and although Benny had his moments and there was never any doubts that the fight wouldn't go the distance, Brown took the verdict. When the pair met again in Leeds three months later, Brown had won the world title to go along with the European and British. In the return Brown was a comfortable winner.

Two years after his win over King who was now British champion, Benny and Johnny were matched again and Thackray failed to get back in the big time when he couldn't repeat his earlier victory in front of his own crowd at Brunswick Stadium where Benny found himself a knockout victim in eight rounds. When the pair met for a fifth time six months later in November 1933 Johnny had won the vacant British bantam title and gone fifteen rounds with Panama Al Brown for the World bantam title in Manchester. (The legend Brown was one of Boxing's freaks. Over six feet tall for a man that boxed at the 8st 6lbs division the Panama boxer seemed to have longer arms than any boxer seen in England before). Benny was counted out in two rounds at Nelson and there was one more fight between the

Battling **Jim Hayes.**

Yorkshireman and Lancastrian. In the last encounter Benny won on a disqualification awarded at Blackpool and in six contests against one of the finest of the era, King had only beaten him three times.

An ageing Jackie Brown was to be the stumbling block to another aspiring Leeds bantam later in the decade when Jimmy Hayes who was always billed as 'Battling Jim Hayes' had three tussles with the legendary flyweight who had moved into the bantam division successfully at first until his old mate 'Kingie' had halted his title challenge. Brown was a veteran of over 120 fights when he stepped into the ring with Hayes for their first meeting in January 1938. In his fight previous, Brown had lost on a disqualification to Len Hampston for the Northern Area title. Desperate to bring the glory back to a flagging career Brown put up a great fight at Leeds Town Hall. There was plenty of leather flying with both men having periods on top. Hayes took the verdict though he had a nasty swelling under the left eye. When the pair met again in the middle of the year in front of Brown's home Manchester crowd, the former world champion had lost his last outing in Glasgow but had beaten Barnsley's Joe Skelly twice. Jackie was known to be hard up and all he'd ever known was boxing. With aggression to the fore Brown displayed all his old class to beat a very tough and plucky Hayes. By the time the two met again for the rubber decider, Hayes was the Northern Area champion after beating Tommy Burns for the title in Leeds. The title which Brown had held in 1936, the year he had moved up from the bantams and then lost in a disqualification to Len Hampston at the Olympia was put up and it proved to be the last championship Jackie Brown would win for his career ended a few months later. Hayes had collected some well known Northern scalps and a second win over Jackie would have been a passage to the eliminator for Johnny King's crown. Brown kept the 4,000 crowd in a state of excitement. It was a vintage Brown who was a clear points winner. Four fights later, war put an end to Brown's career and like the man that took away his world title, Benny Lynch, Brown finished up penniless.

Kid Nicholson, the popular Hunslet bantam.

Another seasoned campaigner of the 1920s was Hunslet born George Kid Nicholson. Managed by Dick Moss and later by Londoner Joe Morris, George belonged to that breed of fighters who had they been fighting in another era would have been a British champion. Originally a flyweight he had fought for the Northern flyweight championship against Billy Hindley at the Free Trade Hall in Manchester in 1924. A disqualification win over Teddy Baldock, the latter's first defeat brought him from the obscurity of a club fighter to the pitch of a title challenger. (The following year Baldock won a version of the World bantamweight championship and in an eighty-fight career, in which he only lost five fights, Baldock was British Bantam champion from 1929-1931.) Johnny Brown was British bantam champion, but because he had been in America, Brown hadn't defended for nearly three years. When Brown turned down the National Sporting Club offer to defend his title because the money was insufficient, the club matched Alf 'Kid' Pattenden and Baldock for the title. There was great rivalry between the two as both came from rival parts of the East End. When Baldock decided the money was not enough, George Nicholson got his chance at the NSC in the summer of 1928.

The Kid had already met Pattenden at London's Premierland and although beaten by a close margin, the Leeds lad was convinced that over the longer twenty round title distance, he could wear Pattenden down. For the first ten rounds Nicholson had it all his own way, his lead being so big the price in Tattersalls was 10-1 on. George was unmarked while his opponent's face was badly swollen. The changing point of the fight came when Pattenden, proving that the many times related story that a fight is never won until the referee raises the victor's hand, caught Nicholson with the do or die sucker punch. Nicholson's over cockiness had proved costly and by the next round Pattenden was champion. Two months later Brown met Baldock in another version of the title, which wasn't recognised by the NSC. The situation was finally resolved when the two claimants, Pattenden and Baldock met in 1929 and Baldock beat his rival over fifteen rounds.

Nicholson's career sagged in the 1930s. He turned down an offer of an Australian tour to stay in the home market. There were some highs. He beat British featherweight champion Johnny Cuthbert avenging a defeat a few years earlier. When his career ended in 1934 Nicholson had lost forty of his 105 fights. Like many others of his era he made nothing from boxing and died penniless some years later.

When the Boxing Board, which had formed in 1929, decided to issue area title belts, Leeds boasted the first Northern Area title winners at both lightweight and middleweight in Jimmy Learoyd and Joe Lowther. Learoyd was reported to have had over 200 fights and fought all the top men in the country at his weight. He won the

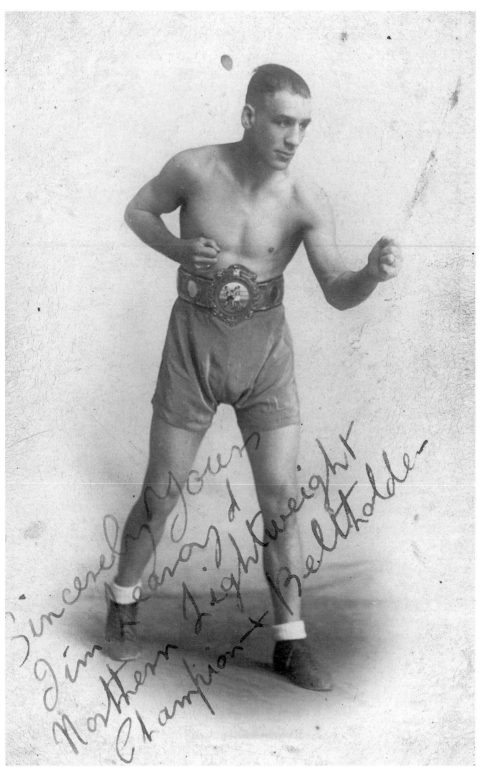

Jimmy Learoyd. Leeds Northern lightweight champion.

Joe Lowther.

Northern Area belt in 1931 beating Ted McGuire at Preston and after retaining his belt against George Lawson at Hull, Jimmy lost it to McGuire at Hull. Two months later he challenged McGuire again and won the rubber 2-1 when McGuire retired in round eleven. His second and last spell as Northern Area champion was ended by Douglas Parker when the referee stopped the action in round fourteen, Parker going onto a title eliminator.

Among the champions Jimmy fought were Al Foreman who was British lightweight champion when he beat Jimmy in 1932. Fred Webster, Harry Corbett whom Jimmy beat in 1934 (Corbett beat Johnny Cuthbert for the lightweight title in 1928 and unsuccessfully challenged for the British bantam and featherweight title). Johnny Curley the featherweight champion in 1930 and Johnny Cuthbert the 'Sheffield Blade' who beat Jimmy in a well remembered fight at Leeds Town Hall. After his retirement Jimmy coached at the St Patrick's Boys Club becoming a professional referee and mine host at the Duke William Inn, Cromwell Street in the 1950s.

Joe Lowther was one of manager Tommy Mallinson's many protégé's and had many classic battles in Leeds. Fighting worthies such as Jack Casey, Charlie McDonald and Fred Shaw. There were also two great tussles against George Cloush, which ended as draws. Lowther won his title in 1930 at Morecambe when he beat Jim Pearson over fifteen rounds and after a second defence against Joe Woodruff at the Olympia in Bradford, Joe was stopped by a great fighter on the way up, Joe Bamford or to give him his boxing name Jack McAvoy 'The Rochdale Thunderbolt'.

Leeds had one of the best featherweights in the North in the thirties in Sonny Lee. Among his impressive victories was Francois Machtens, the Belgian champion. Dick Burke, who gave a good account of himself against Panama Brown and Liverpool Italian, Dom Valante. Sonny also had a very near decision when fighting the classy South African, Louis Bates, when many supporters thought he deserved at least a draw. Many Bradford fans remembered his match with Len Wickwar, the Leicestershire lightweight, at the Olympia in 1936. Wickwar's fight with Sonny was over in the first round. Sonny was counted out because he fell out of the ring and tangled in the press seats.

CHAPTER 12

Boxing in Bradford During the Thirties

The Ted 'Kid' Lewis v Syd Pape Fight

Edwin Holloway's first promotion in 1924 achieved so much notoriety that for the second time in the history of the sport in Bradford, boxing was banned in the town. Special interest in the tournament was aroused when Holloway announced that Ted Kid Lewis, a former World and European Champion, and a winner of over 200 fights was to make his first appearance in Bradford in a match scheduled for fifteen rounds for £100 a side with a weigh in on the day fixed at 12st. His opponent was to be Sergeant Syd Pape from York, who had won respect from the Bradford audience with his appearances against the Australian heavyweight Lloyd.

Rather surprisingly the promotion was a great loss and Holloway had to abandon the only other genuine money match between Young Hoddy and Kid Lambert because takings were so low. The natural assumptions being that the higher prices of admission, necessary to accommodate a boxer of Lewis's standing proved too expensive for the usual fight fans. The result of the fight was that Lewis was in a different class altogether from Pape and immediately opinions were raised whether the fight should have been arranged for it was painfully obvious that the York man had no right at all to be in the same ring as the ex-champion. Lewis handed out the most unmerciful beating and it was amazing to the onlookers that Pape managed to stay on his feet. The fight had hardly been going any length of time when the incensed crowd broke into cries of stopping the fight to save Pape from the bombardment of punches. Referee Harry Jennings came under the most severe criticism for not stopping the fight, the one-sided contest continuing into the second round when Pape's seconds threw the towel in.

To make matters worse seated at the ringside were Alderman

Thomas Sowden, Chairman of the Watch Committee, the Lord Mayor H M Trotter, and the Chief Constable Joseph Ferndale. Rumour has it although the Bradford Press at the time did not say so, that the three guests were splattered with blood from Pape's cuts. The referee Jennings, who bore the brunt of the aftermath criticism, explained he was only carrying out the rules of the game. In a Bradford *Daily Telegraph* interview he stated:

> *That anyone should complain of me not stopping a contest is almost funny. As it happens I have a reputation for being almost too quick in this matter and I daresay I have stopped more contests to save boxers from unnecessary punishment than any referee in the north has. The human element appeals to me always, but fourteen years experience in handling important contests in all parts of the British Isles teaches one to exercise a sense of proportion.*

Harry was quick to announce that Pape was all right soon afterwards.

The Chief Constable was also quick to state his side of the argument. In his opinion it wasn't sport but cruelty, the referee should have stopped the fight or Pape's seconds thrown the towel in before Pape became senseless and battered mercilessly. He also said that the whole affair became sickening and he certainly did not agree with it, and if that was the way boxing was going to be carried on he would do all in his power to stop it being held at the Windsor Hall or any other place for which the corporation is responsible. Other results in what was Bradford's last professional tournament of the 1920s were Jim Learoyd (Leeds) versus Phil Richardson (London) draw. Lew Mosby beat Young Hill (Huddersfield) and Walter Wright (Huddersfield) beat young Fred Delaney.

After the brutality of the Lewis-Pape fight the authorities refused to grant any licences for further professional promotions in the town. Disorderly scenes at a tournament at the Royal Albert Hall had effects of boxing being barred in other areas. Edwin Holloway moved to Hull but was refused admission to run shows there. Surprisingly during the ban, which lasted six years, the sport in the town lost none of its popularity. Amateur boxing which the police took an interest in flourished with several new clubs being admitted to the Northern Counties ABA. Schoolboy boxing with the lead taken by St Bede's and St Joseph's became popular.

Famous Fights at the Olympia, 1930-38

After a six year ban, professional boxing returned to Bradford and the setting was the Olympia buildings near the bottom of Thornton Road for the first bill in the city under the auspices of the Boxing Board of Control, which had promised to clean up the sport, hence the lifting of the ban. A syndicate of Bradford sportsmen under the management of former boxer and now referee Fred Blakeborough were instrumental in putting the first bill together.

Close on 4000 attended the opening night. Prices of 1s 2d, 2s 4d and 3s 6d, with ladies especially invited at 1s 2d to all parts of the hall which were much cheaper than the twenties' charges and by using local talent instead of the previous big names, the policy of cheaper prices meant promotions could be a viable concern.

Leeds man Jimmy Learoyd topped the first bill earning a twelve round points win over Wakefield's Nash Shakespeare, with other wins coming from Mick Melia over Jack Bottomley of Middlesbrough despite giving a lot of weight away. Kid Chocolate Melgram over Tommy Barber and Jack Manley against Silsden's Billy Sullivan. After a few promotions Blakeborough gave way to Harry Haddon. Fred tried to revive boxing at the Windsor Hall afterwards, but was turned down. A drop in audience level saw the venue change from the traditional boxing night of Monday to Saturday and before 1930 was out Albert Heslop from the Leeds National Sporting Club had moved into the promoters chair. Mick Melia was popular on Arthur's bills, earning the plaudits when he beat Bradford's other challenger in the heavier divisions, Ted Brookes. Leeds lads Joe Lowther and Little Minor were also popular and there were very early appearances for the two Hampson boys, Cope and Nipper. (Nipper, real name Len, would later in life challenge for British bantamweight honours).

For the first show in 1931 another new company had moved in headed by Joe McDermott. This time the plan was to engage national known lads as well as the best of the local competition. The best fight on McDermotts opening bill was Little Minor's victory over Jimmy Haddon from Birmingham. McDermott only lasted a couple of weeks and it didn't help when Bradford burglars paid him a visit and took 700 fight tickets, gloves, money and contracts. Kid Kelly, the old Army champion, was the next to try his hand. Kelly reduced admission to 6d and changed the night back to Monday, but then ran into competition with a new venue in Harris Street and, for the time being, boxing was dropped from the Olympia.

In the autumn of 1932 Edwin Holloway returned to Bradford in a promise to bring the big names to the city. A crowd of 4,000 saw his opening bill topper Charlie Smith of Deptford, a leading contender for the British heavyweight title, fight Belgian Peter Van Goole. The Belgian was disappointing and Smith was an easy winner.

Len Harvey v Theo Sas - November 1932

Holloway's promise of the big names brought a 5,000 crowd to the Olympia in November 1932 when Len Harvey, the middleweight champion of Great Britain, made his first appearance in the city. Holloway had gone into partnership with Lawrence Fraser and the appearance of a boxer in Harvey's class aroused great interest. It was another disappointment for another Belgian was not up to the task. Theo Sas, his country's cruiser weight champion, lasted only 175 seconds! Harvey so outclassed his opponent that referee, Jack Smith from Manchester, who had been engaged specially for the bout, had no alternative but to stop it. Harvey apologised to the crowd through the MC and regretted he didn't have more time to show why he had become a champion.

Larry Gains v Marcel Moret - November 1932

If the crowd at the Olympia had thought the Harvey v Sas fight was short, they were in for a shock at the next top of the bill promotion at the stadium a fortnight Later. Holloway and Fraser's next big capture was Larry Gains, the Canadian coloured heavyweight. Gains, who became the British Empire heavyweight champion, was one of the most talked about boxers of the day. Under the management of Harry Levene he had astounded the boxing world by offering to take on Doyle and Pettifer (two of the top heavyweight contenders) on the same night. Gains opponent was Marcel Moret the ex-heavyweight champion of France and now under the wing of Descamps, the ex-manager of Carpentier. To cope with the big crowd, commissioners reinforced the officials and stewards and Holloway had strong barriers especially erected around each division. The affair was very short lived and Gains showed his supremacy by knocking out Moret in only thirty-four seconds. To say the crowd was upset was an understatement. The fifteen three-minute rounds had lasted only thirty-four seconds, and that had included the count. There was severe criticism in the press regarding Moret's worthiness for a fight at championship standards and it certainly appeared to onlookers that he was pounds lighter than Gains. By way of an effort to subdue the catcalls and compensation

Larry Gain's on his visit to Bradford Olympia pays a visit to the *Telegraph & Argus*. The man on the left was the *Telegraph & Argus* Sports Editor at the time Tom Riley.

local heavyweight Ted Brookes stepped into the ring to give an exhibition with the Canadian.

Larry Gains v Bert Casimir - April 1934

Wrestling was as popular as boxing in the 1930s and Holloway became involved with the rival sport, which had proved a big hit on Friday nights at the Olympia. The Boxing Board of Control forbade both sports on the same bill and after only spasmodic boxing promotions the Olympia had new promoters in February 1934 when the Gornalls, Albert and Arthur (father and son) took over and engaged local boxing manager, Jimmy Emmett as matchmaker. Despite the farce of Gains last performance in Bradford, a crowd of 5,000 paid to see the British Commonwealth heavyweight champion's second fight in the city. Gains, who once went seven years without a defeat and held a decision over Primo Carnera (the world champion in 1934) was matched against Bert Casimar, the heavyweight champion of Poland, who claimed he had never been knocked out in his life. International referee Jack Hart was booked to officiate the match which, although it went longer than Gains last fight in Bradford, failed to last longer than the first round. The knockout, which resulted in 125 seconds, was greeted with a show of disapproval and a demand of 'money back'. Hardly a blow was struck in the first minute. Gains was content just to follow Casimir around the ring. When Gains did strike, the Pole concentrated so much on ducking and keeping his head covered which brought instant jeers from the crowd. Although the punch that brought the end seemed crisp enough, Gains had never exerted himself whatsoever.

Tommy Farr v Eddie Pierce - October 1934
The Gornalls returned to the Olympia in October with an international heavyweight match as the bill topper. This second bill Jimmy Emmett was involved with as matchmaker was for him a personal scoop engaging Tommy Farr, the Welsh cruiser weight champion, to fight the South African Champion Eddie Pierce. Farr showed his mettle by winning a points decision despite a broken knuckle in his hand obtained in the third round. It was a pity the fickle Bradford public didn't back Jimmy's judgement, they thought Farr was a thirty bob fighter and the tournament lost money. In less than three years after appearing in Bradford, Farr had become British champion and had gone fifteen rounds in a close decision with Joe Louis for the World heavyweight title.

Jackie Brown v Len Hampston - November 1937
An import of American wrestling champions and the popularity of home based grapplers like Duggie Clark and Jack Pye saw boxing take a back seat and it was not until 1937 that the Olympia had a major promotion. Promoter Jack Green's justification in choosing the Olympia instead of Leeds proved successful when a packed house turned out to see former world flyweight champion Jackie Brown and Batley fighter Len Hampston, who had won previous disqualification awards against Benny Lynch and European champion, Maurice

OLYMPIA HALL
Thornton Road, Bradford.

MONDAY, OCTOBER 17th, 1932
FIRST CONTEST AT 7-45.

PROMOTER—
Mr. L. FRASER, B.B.B.C.
Manager—Mr. E. E. HOLLOWAY, B.B.B.C.
PRICE TWOPENCE

Dubois of Switzerland fight for the Northern bantam title. The fight got off to a sensational start when, in the first few seconds, Brown was down for a count of eight. After surviving the first round despite being stuck in the corner receiving blow after blow, Brown recovered enough to put on a spirited display. When Hampston came back with a strong challenge in the thirteenth and the former World champion was subject to a battering of body blows, Brown rushed his opponent to the ropes and proceeded to halt Hampston by persistent holding from which he received a disqualification. After the Yorkshireman had been declared the winner, it was revealed he was very lucky to have appeared in the ring, he was apparently struck down with a mystery pain only an hour before the fight.

Kid Tanner v Jim Hayes - December 1938

Hampston topped the bill again in January 1938 and was beaten by Frenchman Bernard Leroux when Jack Green wanted him for this third Olympia promotion. Len Announced he was retiring so Green substituted Leeds boxer Jim Hayes to fight Kid Tanner, the bantam and featherweight champion from British Guinea. Before proceedings Johnny King the British champion was introduced in the ring and it was stated King would fight Tanner at the Olympia in 1939 for the British Empire bantam title. The Tanner-Hayes fight was a spectacular affair with Tanner. King's fight with Tanner didn't take place and boxing had to take a back seat for Britain had a fight of its own to contend.

CHAPTER 13

Bradford Boxing Characters from the 1930s

Fred Shaw

Bradford thought it had a future middleweight champion at the beginning of the 1930s when Fred Shaw produced the performance of his life to beat Marcel Thil, The European champion, at 11st 6lbs, but alas Fred could not live up to his early expectations.

Young Shaw had commenced his boxing career at Hanson School and a spare bedroom over his father's pub, the *Golden Lion* at Laisterdyke, was his first training centre. One of the city's dedicated enthusiasts, Pat Smith, an ex-Army instructor put him through his paces and among other Bradford lads who attended Smith's sessions were flyweight Chris Green, Ted Brookes, The Barbers Jack and Tommy, and Charlie Fudd. Fred was a popular competitor at the annual Police tournaments promoted by the West Riding Constabulary at the Victoria Hall. In 1924 he reached the open lightweight final only to be narrowly defeated by Arthur Jones of Liverpool. After winning the Northern Counties junior welterweight championship, Fred was to put an unbeaten run together in the

Marcel Thil the French world champion who was beaten by Fred Shaw.

A meeting of the now defunct ex Bradford Boxers Association. Sitting round the tables are **Jim Mahoney**, **Fred Shaw** and Bradford flyweight **Chris Green**.

amateur rankings. In 1926 at Shipley he was a popular winner over Pat McIvenney, the Irish Guards champion, and when the Police again invited several Irish amateur champions over the following year Fred's opponent was Guarda Cooper, the welter champion. The two had met previously and had boxed a draw in Ireland. After suffering a bad eye injury, Fred changed his tactics and reversed the course of the fight to win acclaim for a great victory. As expected Fred turned professional in 1928, a fact that at one time looked impossible as it looked as if he wouldn't recover from a bad attack of scarlet fever when he was a youngster. One of his last fights as an amateur was at Wakefield Drill Hall when he beat Constable Barnes, the police welterweight champion of England.

At the age of about twenty since joining the paid ranks, Fred had made rapid strides. His only defeat was against Jim Pearson of Preston at Leeds. The loss was hotly disputed, but there was no mistake in the return for Fred won every round. His highly acclaimed victory over Thil at Manchester Free Trade Hall brought Shaw's name forward as the most promising middleweight in the country. Until his defeat Thil had put a great unbeaten run together and among his victims were Joe Bloomfield, Ted Moore, and Europeans Orlando Leopardi and Marcel Thuru. In fact up to Thil winning the world championship in 1932 his defeat by Fred was his only loss in five years and he went on to hold his World title for the next five years, defending it successfully on eight occasions. As already stated Fred could not reach the same heights again. Two defeats at the hands of Mileke Libert in Belgium in a fortnight when he was severely criticised by the press for 'a lack of devil'. A loss against Pierre Gaudon at the Bal Bullier boxing club in Paris, and another against the Dutchman Van Vleit, whom he had previously beaten in Amsterdam destroyed his ambitions of big money on the European circuit. Even his appearances in England did not put him back on the winning run. A change of tactic when he threw aside his previous immaculate defence for more aggression proved to no avail and during the next couple of years he dropped several decisions. Joe Lowther beat him twice, as did Charlie McDonald who won the best of three. A chance to step back into the bigtime came when he fought Len Harvey, the British middleweight champion in a non-title bout at the Kings Hall, Belle Vue proved disastrous when Fred was knocked out in the third round. Fred carried on for a few years later, still able to command top of the bill money at local events, and due to the demand of the boxing boom appearing a lot more regularly than he should have done. At the time of his death in the early 80s, he was a nightwatchman at a textile mill.

Pat Delaney
The big surprise of 1933 was when Mitchell Gill easily Bradford's top wrestler turned to boxing. Gill, the son of a Manningham coal merchant, had been a wrestler for five years. He was thought to have a great future in the sport and several promoters had put him in the championship class. A meeting with Larry Gains and his manager convinced Gill he could make his name as a boxer. Choosing a name strongly associated with boxing in Bradford; he made his debut at the Royal Albert Hall on the Harvey v Peterson bill, and easily beat Archie Norman of Hampstead. After winning another fight at the Hall and one at the Olympia in London against Bill Partridge of

Poplar, he made his boxing debut in Bradford accompanied by his manager Harry Levene, he won another short fight over George Taylor of Hull. Two days later he returned to the 'Albert' to win his fifth fight beating Jack Kealey of Birmingham. Wrestling wasn't given up altogether. He returned to the Bradford Olympia as Mitchell Gill in November 1934. Wrestling was at its height of popularity in the mid-thirties and Gill, with boxing promotions very spasmodic at the Thornton Road venue, resumed his top of the bill wrestling status.

The White Abbey Boys - Mick and John Melia

The Melia brothers, Mick and John, came to live in the White Abbey district of Bradford as boys from Ireland. Both boxed as middleweights and above and both were members of Jimmy Emmet's management stable, as was Chris Green the Canterbury estate flyweight, Jackie Quinn and Bill Bartley.

Mick was good enough to represent the England ABA teams in Ireland when he gave a sparkling display in beating Ian Miller, the Irish welterweight champion. Turning pro under Jimmy he was a winner on the first Olympia bill and was unbeaten in his first seven fights, his victims including Sergeant Jordan and Sam McVea of York. Considered the best fight ever staged at Harrogate Skating Rink, Mick fought his most memorable fight against Jim Learoyd with whom he had one or two battles. Referee O'Brien delayed his decision apparently to make a few remarks, which annoyed the crowd thinking the result, was going to be a draw demonstrated with instant booing. Then afterwards it was apparent that proceedings had got out of hand when the referee announced that if anyone wished to insult him all he had to do was climb in the ring. Despite vigorous protests

the decision was given to the Leeds man Learoyd. The result so annoyed poor Jimmy Emmett that in the interests of the fighter he himself went to the ringside to protest and offer himself out to the referee over six rounds!

John Melia's career was mostly on small hall promotions and his most famous fight never happened in a ring. Like many other boxers on retiring from the ring who took jobs as barmen or stewards at dance halls and clubs, John worked for a while as doorman at the Textile Hall at the bottom of White Abbey and was also engaged at *The Angel* at Morley which was always a focal

Big John Melia.
Bradford man who tackled a rugby team.

point for entertainment and punters travelled distances for a night out there. One incident happened there that made John famous the length and breadth of Yorkshire. The story becoming a talking point in pubs and clubs for so many years that the tale became legend. One of John's lifetime friends wrote about the event and labelled it 'The Leeds Massacre':

> *A full rugby team he battered one night*
> *There are witnesses living who saw that great fight*
> *Thirteen big giants all raring to go.*
> *He hammered the lot of them, God what a show,*
> *And they didn't come single but all in a rush.*
> *Johnny Melia fought on, in the midst of the crush.*
> *He butchered them all with fist and with head.*
> *As they lay on the floor people thought some were dead.*
> *BIG JOHN stood there grinning and straightening his hair*
> *Said "Count them all Harry, I think they're all there".*
> *As ambulances came to take them away*
> *BIG JOHN just laughed and said "What a great day"*

John moved to Blackpool for the last thirty years of his life and among many of his engagements was bodyguard to the singer Joseph Locke.

The Ted Brookes v Primo Carnera Exhibition Fight - 1931

Promoter Jack Smith pulled off a scoop by engaging World heavyweight champion Primo Carnera to visit England to fight a series of exhibition matches in early 1931. Three appearances were fixed for Liverpool, Morecambe and Manchester and Smith drew up a list of boxers all over six foot tall which he shortened to a possible half dozen, to go into the ring with the Italian, including Bradford's Ted Brookes. Three opponents were engaged at each venue to go two rounds of two-minute duration. Ted, who weighed 14st and stood 6ft 2in, got his chance at Morecambe Winter Gardens, when as well as taking on three heavyweights Carnera entertained the crowd by pretending to be scared of 4ft 6in flyweight Kid Furness. Brooke's performance was marred when he accidentally got caught by a terrific blow and was sent flying across the ring. When interviewed afterwards Ted said:

> *I would not go into the ring with him again for a fortune if I thought I was going to get another like that. It was like being kicked by a mule. He is a great fellow but he hits too hard.*

Ted Brookes, the Bradford heavyweight

Ted Brookes in exhibition against world champion Primo Carnera, at the Winter Gardens, Morecambe in 1931. This photograph was, for years, featured in Ted's pea and pie shop in Otley Road.

Ted received a contract to box Carnera again the following year in Ireland, which was withdrawn, when Carnera took another fight and didn't make the trip. Long after he retired Ted had a pea and pie shop in Otley Road and a photo of his match against Carnera was featured in his shop window.

Bradford Promoter John McDermott travelled to London to interview Carnera's manager. There was a demand for a fight between Primo and Islas Epifanio and 'Mac' had hopes of holding the match at an open-air tournament at Valley Parade. Although Carnera's backers showed interest in the match it never took place

CHAPTER 14

Keighley Boxing Characters from the 1930s

Freddie Irving

The big crowd puller at Keighley Drill Hall in the early thirties was young Freddie Irving. Jack Dempsey was every schoolboy's idol and Freddie was no exception. When the champion's million dollar boxing extravaganzas were hitting the headlines, Irving was an avid listener. It wasn't long before Freddie was emulating his idol in the ring.

After schoolboy appearances whilst still at St Anne's, Freddie was only fifteen when he signed up with Keighley boxing manager and promoter Sam Scaife. He was still fifteen when he stepped into the ring at the Drill Hall on 5 January 1930, to meet another Keighley

boy, Billy Holmes, over six rounds. After winning his first fight on points, Freddie returned to the same hall a fortnight later to repeat the decision over Batley's Jim Whitworth. Freddie's next two fights were at Horton Green Social Club, which was above the old Prince's Theatre in Bradford. Freddie's devastating punching saw him put his first opponent, Young Dunn, down for several counts in a points win, whilst his second appearance saw him deliver a knockout punch to Shaw.

In 1933 **Freddie Irving** had the satisfaction of avenging one of his early defeats when, in front of his supporters, he out-pointed Irishman Bobby Traynor. The pair are pictured here at the weigh-in, with Freddie on the left.

Irving's performance must have been memorable because afterwards a local vicar objected and the club was shut!

After three more fights in which he stayed unbeaten, Freddie suffered his first defeat when fighting at eight rounds for the first time. Young Aldridge, one of Leeds's most promising bantams, beat him over the distance. In August 1930, the Keighley youngster made his debut at Bradford's premier boxing venue of the time, The Olympia. His opponent was an equally promising youngster from Bradford called Johnny Quinn. Boosted by the help of his father, a local promoter, Quinn had built up an unbeaten reputation at local venues. Not to be overawed in front of a partisan crowd and boxing with a class well in advance of his years, Irving put up a great performance to end Quinn's unbeaten run.

Back at the Drill Hall Freddie was matched with one of Keighley's most colourful fighters, Crossflatt's Percy Vear. Percy, himself no slouch in the ring, failed to halt Irving's progress and already some of the sport's followers were predicting great things for the youngster. In December of the first year of his boxing career, Freddie met Bobby Traynor, the Irish Free State bantam champion. It was obvious that Irving was not ready for a fighter of Traynor's class and he was beaten on points after surviving a count of eight. Benny Green, who had refereed the fight, was impressed enough by the lad's performance to secure him bookings at his brother's hall, the Brunswick Stadium, and Leeds National Sporting Club, the top venues in Leeds.

Boxing as a bill topper for the first time in front of his own crowd, and for the first time at ten rounds, Freddie delighted the Keighley fans when he put paid to Burnley's Norman Beckett's run of twenty-five unbeaten fights. From the Beckett fight he quickly strung together a run of ten undefeated matches, including a trip to Workington where he defeated the local champion Jack Hewson, who himself had been unbeaten for twenty-three fights.

It was around this time that a telegram arrived in Keighley asking if Freddie could make a match in Royton the following Sunday against a World champion, Al Brown. 'Panama' Al Brown, as he was better known, had been World champion since 1929 and was on a European tour meeting the best men in the lower weight division. Leeds boxer Sonny Lee had been due to meet the champion but had become indisposed and the promoter obviously aware of Freddie's growing reputation, offered the youngster the fight at a specified weight. To be invited to appear in the ring with a world champion was an honour in itself but Scaife was reluctant, where other unscrupulous promoters would have had no qualms, to put a lad of seventeen in the ring at that stage of his career against the much more experienced world champion.

Percy Vear, whom Freddie had beaten in one of his early fights had himself been producing excellent form in his matches at the Drill Hall and the local promoters, knew they were onto a good thing when they re-matched the pair. The match captured the Keighley fans' imagination and it stirred memories of some of Tommy Rowan's early fights in the town. Former British middleweight champion Tommy Gummer was chosen to officiate the fight which was fixed for £25 a side and there was a lot of money laid out in Keighley as each set of supporters wanted to bet on their man. So much so, that around the George Street area, it was rumoured that some of the locals had practically pawned their houses on the result. Poor Percy had to make a determined effort to get down to the weight, which turned out to be to no avail as Freddie repeated his previous victory.

Freddie became a big favourite at the Imperial Ballroom, Nelson where he was never beaten. He was regularly fighting twelve rounders and in March 1933 was matched with one of the best men in Leeds, at the ballroom. Sonny Lee held a decision over British featherweight champion Seaman Watson, who was then fighting in America for the world title. In one of his best remembered fights, Freddie beat the well fancied Lee on points. Freddie outpointed one of his early victors, Bobby Traynor at Keighley, but lost the re-match with Lee.

In September, acting as a substitute at twenty-four hours notice, Freddie took on Jimmy Walsh of Chester. Despite a creditable performance against the man who in a couple of years was British lightweight champion. Irving was beaten on points. A month later there was another clash with Lee, this time in the Brunswick in Lee's hometown. Despite having Lee down he had to settle for a very disappointing draw which caused an early rumpus among the Keighley supporters.

Early in 1934, Freddie left Sam Scaife with the record of 68 fights and only twelve defeats, all of them fought as a teenager. Freddie signed for Billy Bridgewater, the Doncaster promoter and manager of British boxing champions Roland Todd and Harry Crossley. Sadly he failed to live up to a brilliant future which looked assured after his early performances in Keighley and it was not long before he drifted out of the fight scene.

Johnny Barratt

The main rival to Freddie Irving in the 1930s for the title 'best boxer' in Keighley was Johnny Barratt. Although they were of completely different styles, Barratt being more the stylist and Irving the boxer, their meeting would have meant a classic confrontation but the pairing never came off.

Johnny Barratt was one of the many Keighley boxers who had his boxing lessons while still at St Anne's School, winning his way to the final of the NC schoolboy competition at Saltaire. Johnny met another St Anne's boxer in Jimmy Rowan; son of Keighley's first boxing idol Tommy Rowan. Although he was beaten, Johnny got his revenge the following week at Keighley Drill Hall. Johnny did become a schoolboy champion and it was not long after in October 1928, that he met Tommy Briggs at Keighley in his professional debut and started with a win. Sam Scaife was the main man in boxing in Keighley during the late twenties and thirties as well as manager of most of Keighley's boxers he was also the town's promoter. Scaife and his associates duly recognised Johnny's talents and gave him a chance to appear on the local bills.

Barratt's first full season as a professional saw him fight eleven times of which he only lost two. The following year, 1930, out of his eleven contests he won seven, drew two and lost three. One of his reversals being against Percy Vear at Workington.

In 1931 Johnny had a disastrous time managing only three wins out of his fourteen bouts. One defeat being against Young Aldridge of Leeds who had also beaten Fred Irving. The following year with a greater concentration on training, Johnny was able to shake off his bad spell to such an extent that the only defeat in 1932 out of seventeen fights was against Joe Cowley at Goldthorpe in a ten rounder.

From his early fights Johnny had now graduated to top of the bill. Barratt commenced 1933 just where he had left off in 1932 and since the Cowley defeat he remained unbeaten in his next twenty-three fights, beating such men as Leeds boxers Billy Shaw and Billy Miller in the process. His phenomenal run caught the eye of the top promoters and in October at Brunswick Stadium (Leeds) he became the first Keighley boxer to meet a reigning British champion over twelve rounds, although it wasn't a championship fight. He had taken part in almost 100 fights in five years and this was his first occasion at three-minute rounds. There was a good sprinkling of Keighley supporters in the audience for Jack Green's battle of the roses between Johnny and Johnny King the British and Empire bantam champion.

The first two rounds were fairly even with Barratt matching King in ring technique. The next two rounds were clearly Barratt's who cleverly outboxed the champion. King came back in the fifth to take the round, although some of the crowd was of the opinion that one of King's punches landed low. Johnny's performance in the first half of the fight caused the champion to change tactics and from the fifth he adopted a more aggressive role. King's severe punching caused Barratt to back off and thereby the course of the fight changed. In the seventh Johnny took two counts of eight. The champion's low feints, which had opened the Keighley man's guard, gave the impression he was hitting low and after Johnny had fallen the crowd began to demonstrate their disapproval which carried on to the end. By the eighth it was over. King's strong finishing saw Johnny fall again and counted out. His spirited display especially in the early rounds gained him a standing ovation. Johnny King lost his title in 1934, regained it the following year and was champion for another twelve years until Jackie Patterson beat him in twelve rounds in 1947. Percy Vear appeared on the Barratt v King bill and helped restore some of Keighley's pride when he went the distance with Manchester's Bob Caulfield.

When Keighley welcomed their hero home the following month at the Drill Hall, Johnny suffered another setback when Leeds boxer Benny Thackray beat him and the second defeat was followed by another, this time at the hands of Arthur Killeen of Bolton. The King fight had proved Johnny's peak and he never boxed with the same consistency again. In 1934 he only won nine of seventeen fights, with one of his defeats coming against Ronnie James who, a decade later was British champion and a World title contender.

Johnny Barratt's career lasted for quite a few more years and there was a well remembered competition at the Drill Hall in which he beat Baz Rawton in the final. He was even boxing during the war when as a member of the home guard he fought Tommy Miller at the Princess Hall, Bingley.

Never the sensationalist but having pure boxing ability, Johnny was a master of self defence, it was only his weak point, a lack of stamina, that stopped him from a career at the top. A firm favourite of the purist not only in Keighley but also in venues all over the country.

Percy Vear
Sam Scaife used to carry a publicity card in his pocket headlining the talent of three aces. Johnny Barrett and Freddie Irving were two; the third was Percy Vear. Perhaps overshadowed by the other two locally,

Percy proved to be a bill topper in his own right up and down the country. Born in Crossflatts in 1911, Percy first caught the eye of former Bingley boxer Harry Chester. Moving to Sam Scaife's management in the later 1920s, Percy commenced a boxing career which, in the following years, soon topped over a hundred appearances in the ring.

Boxing as a bantam and later as a featherweight the demand of the boxing boom proved so hectic that going on for thirty fights a year were the norm for ringmen like Percy Vear who never let anybody down, often appearing as a late substitute. He was over-matched in some quite bruising fights, but win or lose he always gave his best.

Quite early in his career, he took part in a great six round match with another Keighley youngster. One of the best fights ever staged between two Keighley boxers, the big shame was that not many locals were able to witness it, for the venue was Workington and the other Keighley boxer was Johnny Barratt. The Workington press called it the best match ever staged in the area and Percy was

Percy Vear, one of Keighley's best.

judged a close winner. A couple of months later Vear met Freddie Irving in the ring. Young Haggas was billed to fight Irving, his unavailability saw Percy step in and the result was a match that had the crowd on the edge of their seats. Freddie won but Percy made him work hard to get the decision. After the Irving fight, Percy began a winning run that proved the most successful of his fight career. Unbeaten in his next fifteen fights, his victories including wins over Kid Close of Leeds who had only lost five out of sixty odd fights and Jackie Quinn, a fighter with a reputation in Bradford. There was a draw with Mick Howard of Liverpool at Wigan. The fight had been so one sided that even the Lancastrians demonstrated in favour of a Yorkshireman following the referee's decision.

The run of wins put Percy Vear's name at the top of the bill and soon he was in demand to fight boxers in other areas. As such he went to Sheffield and took on Dixie Inkles one of the steel city's top small men. Over 7,000 witnessed the open air promotion which saw a great fight lasting thirteen rounds. Percy had him swaying on the ropes several times, but seasoned campaigner Inkles knew enough about in-fighting to take the decision. Although the unbeaten run had finished, Percy had found a new bunch of admirers in South Yorkshire and he began to appear regularly in the area. He beat Jack Skelly one of Barnsley's best men and won, and drew with Inkles great rival Steve Firman of Swinton. Another match with Inkles was certain after the first fight and the pair topped the bill at Attercliffe at a tournament promoted by Jack Cuthbert, father of British champion Johnny. Revenge was sweet for Percy took the decision, the result of which virtually put an end to Inkles' claims for a title fight.

Percy's form began to suffer in the next twenty or so matches, his inconsistency meaning he won only half of his bouts, his victories including one over Silsden's Billy Sullivan.

To wind up the 1932 season and to settle local arguments Percy and Freddie Irving were matched a second time at the Drill Hall. Irving was still only seventeen but not far off the peak of his career. Nearly 1,400 packed the Drill Hall that night in the first genuine big money fight in Keighley for many years. Percy, as usual, fought to his limit but there was no stopping Irving that night and he took the points decision. There were still more victories for Percy but his form suffered so much that he only won one of his last fifteen fights, the demands of the thirties boom taking its toll, Percy was finally forced to give up his livelihood, which in a later era would have been much less demanding and much more rewarding.

Arthur Barnes

Sharing a billing with Irving and Barratt in the Keighley boxing halls was Arthur Barnes who, after reverting to amateur status, only returned to the professional ring after suffering a personal tragedy.

Arthur was born in Workington in 1903, a member of a large Cumberland family of fourteen children. Two of his elder brothers, Jack and George, were boxers but before he could follow in their footsteps the First World War put a stop to both brother's careers. It was as a private in the 5th Border Regiment that young Barnes first donned boxing gloves and it was not long before his potential was realised and he was appearing in Army championships. To coin a quip from an elderly boxing bill 'Battling Barnes' made so much progress that by 1922 he had appeared at the National Sporting Club and emerged as winner of the 42nd East Lancashire Territorial's bantamweight competition.

Arthur Barnes.

2

Wharncliffe Books
FREEPOST SF5
47 Church Street
BARNSLEY
South Yorkshire
S70 2BR

Mr/Mrs/Ms ....

Address ....

....

.... Postcode ....

E-mail address ....

Trade enquiries please tick []   Telephone: 01226 734555

I am particularly interested in - please tick special interest areas:

Aspects Series	[]	Transport History	[]
Industrial History	[]	Entertainment (Theatre & Cinema)	[]
Local Interest	[]	Places to Visit	[]

About this time he followed one of his sisters and moved to Keighley. Eventually taking a job on the railway a position he'd held in Cumbria. Training sessions at Leeds were quickly followed by the signing of professional forms under Leeds manager Tommy Oates. For his first pro outing he was matched against British champion Joe Fox in a six round exhibition. Young Barnes was not overawed and put up a creditable performance against a man who was worthy of a crack at the world title. The week after he had his first full fight and was narrowly beaten on points by Alf Butters of Goldthorpe. Very quickly graduating from six rounds to ten round contests, Arthur was matched with Billy Armer of Lancaster at the Boxing Stadium, Mill Street, Leeds. Armer had a long list of credentials including the title of champion of all India 1921-22 and the winner of over 100 fights. After one round Armer had had enough, Arthur's explosive punching causing the Lancastrian's handlers to throw in the towel. Arthur quickly became a favourite in Leeds, and appearing regularly at the Sporting Club in Templar Street, he duly completed inside the distance wins over Joe Conn whom he beat twice, Young Kenny of Manchester and Young Malloy of Leeds. The Leeds Sunday afternoon crowd was in for a treat in Arthur's next appearance in the city. His opponent was George Clark, a Londoner who had won several competitions in France. Aggression ruled the day and Arthur came out a points winner after fierce exchanges. Arthur's next fight was in front of the knowledgeable crowd at Liverpool where he defeated the Welsh lightweight champion Arthur Davies. Barnes's run of victories came to an end when he was beaten by Wakefield's Harry Norton at Leeds.

In the middle twenties, Arthur became disillusioned with the professional game and with the help of superintendent Coates who did so much for boxing in Keighley dropped from the paid ranks and was re-instated as an amateur. Joining the Airedale Boxing Club, he quickly came to prominence in 1927 by winning the NC Lightweight title at Saltaire. Unfortunately he was unable to travel to the Royal Albert Hall for the national ABA finals.

By the end of the year he returned to professional status, the circumstances largely being decided by a fire, which wiped out all his personal possessions and left him only with the clothes he stood in. His re-appearance saw him matched with Billy Allen at Salford who, despite a great performance, was beaten on points. Back on a winning trail, Arthur's next two fights were at Preston when he beat Stan Bradbury and drew with Vic Maudsley. There were also appearances at Todmorden Drill Hall where he knocked out Ted

Horsfall of Leeds and fought two classic encounters with Huddersfield's George Beaumont. On both occasions Beaumont was given the verdict and the crowd demonstrated against them both. Dewsbury Socialist Club was the scene of Arthur's next action and poor Hector Wilbie of Goole was the opponent who failed to last one round.

Arthur's next match was a special occasion. He was invited back to Workington to take part in a boxing tournament promoted by his old regiment. His opponent was to be his mentor from his early boxing days in the Army, Sergeant Major J McQuiggan. The local Workington paper played up the story of the master versus pupil confrontation, especially as Arthur had commenced his career in the town. Arthur stated that because of promotion on the railway and not having the available time, the Workington fight was to be his last. Fighting for the first time over fifteen rounds, Arthur put up a great display and although the crowd was on the major's side, the decision got the nod of approval. Both boxers were given a standing ovation, which lasted long after the fight.

The enforced retirement due to his job did not take place and a month later he appeared on Harry Chester's promotion at Bingley Drill Hall. Topping the bill Arthur was to have met Mike Maloney of Doncaster, who did not appear. Rather than disappoint the local fans he met the heavier Tiger Smith who was easily tamed inside the distance.

Keighley had not seen a boxing show for a few seasons and when Sam Scaife decided to take the plunge by holding a show at the Keighley Athletic Club at West Lane (Lords Buildings) in September 1928, he plumped for Arthur as his first bill topper. The promotion was a big success and Arthur produced the goods by giving as good as he got against Castleford's Albert Jarvis, a leading lightweight with a knock out reputation. Arthur had been down twice and although Jarvis recovered sufficiently the referee's decision of a draw brought hoots of disapproval. The result was a natural re-match and was an obvious gate puller for the next promotion. The rebirth of Keighley boxing on his shoulders, Arthur got the decision this time beyond doubt, bombarding Jarvis with punches from all angles, he and one and all were surprised how Jarvis hung on. At the end of the night, the promoters fully flushed with success announced they were negotiating for a larger hall. Four days after the Jarvis fight, Barnes took a fight with Len Tiger Smith, the Midlands champion and a title contender, when despite a hand injury he was narrowly beaten on points.

Promoter Sam Scaife with Arthur's assistance commenced boxing at the Drill hall in Keighley in November 1928 and naturally Arthur topped the bill. It was a disappointment for the local man, desperate to deliver the goods. Arthur brought his opponent to his knees. The victim who was Len Brown of Rotherham claimed a foul, which the referee sanctioned, leaving Arthur disqualified after only two rounds. The defeat was soon forgotten and Arthur won his next two fights at the hall.

Irishman Mike Maloney a veteran of over 100 fights and holder of the Northern Counties Welterweight title threw out a challenge to the man who had beaten him two years earlier, and the match was set for the next Keighley promotion. Maloney turned up but a broken nose prevented him from entering the ring. With him was his stablemate, Ike Hardy, a victor over Maloney and again a bigger and heavier man. Not to disappoint the crowd, Arthur stepped in to fight Hardy but he had set himself a man's job. Barnes carried the fight for the first four rounds; his powerful punching had the crowd thinking of another home win. In the next round they witnessed a sight they hadn't seen before, Barnes on the floor and twice in one round at that. He was not beaten yet and came back the following round to put Hardy on his seat. In the next he had the chance of finishing the bout, for after one or two rushes he caught his man two wicked hooks to the jaw and could have sent him flying through the ropes. He lifted his man to the centre of the ring, an action not unnoticed by the fans and stood back to let his opponent regain his balance. This probably cost him the fight for Hardy recovered to take the verdict on points. Referee Pat Smith said that in the whole of twenty-one year's experience he had never seen a finer example of sportsmanship, a point that the crowd fully appreciated to the extent of a standing ovation.

Arthur's next fight was back in Workington where he suffered his first knockout after seventy-three contests. The victor was a young up and coming Horace Moses. Barnes was beaten in his next two fights, both points decisions to Al Mulrooney of Macclesfield and both at open air events at Harrogate. The return attracting a crowd of over 1,000. Over 800 people turned up at Sam Scaife's next Drill Hall promotion after it was announced Arthur was retiring and would bow out in front of his own crowd. A broken nose was causing breathing difficulties and an operation was needed. In four rounds the fight was over, Batley's John Cassidy being unable to continue.

Old fighters do not lie down and Barnes returned to the ring meeting two of the best men in the area in Nash Shakespeare and

Jimmy Lumb. At the end of the 1931 season he was matched against Tom Larkin of Sheffield. Only eighteen Larkin had lost twice and reversed both defeats. Arthur, ten years older, was making another return to the ring after being out of action for a nose operation. They were labelling Larkin the 'Jack Dempsey of Sheffield'. Arthur proved he was no pushover by forcing the youngster to retire in six rounds. Arthur's career was drawing to a close and he finally retired for good to make way for 'up and comers'.

Bill Sedgwick

During the thirties' boxing boom, Skipton produced several fighting men to rival the Irvings and Vears back down the valley, none more prominent than Bill Sedgwick, who had to travel south to try and find his fame in the boxing ring.

Bill had done a bit of spar boxing with school pals before taking his first progressive steps in the sport by joining the Keighley Amateur club at seventeen. Arthur Barnes was the local king pin and the young Skipton boy felt privileged to trade sparring punches with the local hero, Billy Robinson 'Steeton's pride' was another at the same club with a good amateur record.

Sedgwick worked in a shop in those days, but that wasn't good enough for him. He did not finish until 7.00pm and this interfered with his boxing so he left and took a job in the painting trade for a time. Billy Wiggin, one of Skipton's top boxers and Nelson born Ted Shorrocks were Billy's contemporaries in Skipton and the trio spent

practically every night in a dimly lit gym learning their craft.

Bill's career commenced in 1925 and boxing around the local venues for the next year or so, he won nearly all his fights. In October 1927 he entered a lightweight competition at Premierland, one of the top three London venues. Word had got out that Bill had walked from Skipton to London to participate. The news was in the press and the MC on the night, Buster Cohen, even gave it out that this was the case.

Bill won his first competition beating Gunner Joy on points sharing £15 noblings with his opponent. (Noblings was money thrown into the ring to show

Bill Sedgwick, the Skipton man who walked to London.

appreciation of a good fight). The fact that he had come down to London on a ten shilling day ticket and had been pressurised into saying he had walked for publicity purposes played on the youngster's mind and twelve months to the day, he did walk to London for a fight. Catching the train to Bradford he left his bag at Dewsbury with the local promoters at 4:30pm on Thursday, and arrived in London twenty-four hours later, going straight to the promoter's office where he was fighting the next day. The promoter took him to his home, for as well as being tired young Sedgwick had contracted a cold. It was bed until 8pm on the fight night and to end the story in Bill's own words: 'I won, but I must have been mad. I felt better about walking to London. It was not a lie anymore'.

While in London, Bill went to the International Gym in Dean Street, which was the rendezvous for managers and promoters, and after half a round ring display the Skipton boxer had the choice of three managers. From the choice of Frank Burns, Johnny Hughes (who had fought Jimmy Wilde for a world title) and F H Bunster, young Billy picked the latter. Bunster came from South America with a boxer matched against British featherweight champion, John Curley, and decided to stay in Britain. Bunster was a rare breed amongst boxing managers. For a start he was university educated and secondly he was straight with his boxers. Billy signed for seven years but the affair only lasted three months. Rival managers complained to the Board of Trade that Bunster was taking away their living and as a result his work permit was taken away.

While living in Bunster's flat Billy had London experience boxing in the booths and the competition, which had been the beginning of his London career. Billy progressed to the final and as his opponent failed to turn up he was announced the winner. Fighting from the capital in the next few months he beat Joe Mansell (three rounds), Geo Thompson (Two rounds), Ben Leva (two rounds) and also won a fifteen round points contests against Kid Summers, the lightweight champion of India. There were also two clashes with Harry Sullivan, one a draw, the other a twelve round defeat.

Covent Gardener Gus Warman had returned from America with the reputation of a first round knockout specialist. He was booked to fight Fred Dyer (the singing boxer, a Welshman known in Bradford for his fights with Fred Delaney) at Premierland. Dyer had to pull out and recommended Bill as his last minute substitute. Top of the bill was British champion Jack Hood. Boxing news reported that the champion was disappointing and the support bout was much brighter. The report ran

> *Gus Warman somehow gained the favourable report of Jack Hart over
> Bill Sedgwick of Skipton. I made the Yorkshire lad in front and could
> quite understand the booing Jack received.*

They wanted a return the following week and rather than miss the
chance Bill took the fight even though he had three fights in the week
already booked. Fighting his fourth fight in four days, Bill climbed
into the ring with Warman and at the halfway stage he was rocking
the Cockney with left hooks. Warman came back as his opponent
tired and at the bell the Skipton lad was lucky to be on his feet.

Billy finished his 1928 campaign losing only five of his twenty-
three contests. He beat Harry Sullivan at their third meeting and to
prove his mastery beat him again the following month. As well as
appearing at Premierland, there were appearances at The Ring,
Blackfriars, the working man's venue. Also during the year he had
valuable experience by sparring with Teddy Baldock, the British
bantam champion.

In 1929 he boxed regularly in the south and built up a list of
victories including among his victims Dagenham's Billy Peters, the
ex-London ABA champion, Marine Bartran and Kid Roberts. In
April he defeated Mick Morris at Bournemouth in the opening
round of the South of England welterweight championship which
meant a gold belt for the winner. He beat Morris in two rounds and
progressed to the semi-finals, but was told his fight had been put
back a week and when he did not appear at the first date his
opponent, the Midlands entrant, got a bye into the final. The
following year he continued his good form but came unstuck against
Reg Day, the Eastern Counties lightweight champion, who beat him
in a hard ten rounder. There was a creditable draw with George
Rumsey, who went fifteen rounds with Seaman Tommy Watson the
British champ later.

Johnny Walker, who was just starting to make his name as a
promoter, offered Sedgwick a fight with Jerry Sands who had just
beaten the lightweight champion of France at the National Sporting
Club. A fight had been arranged with Sands before and he had not
turned up, and when Sands blobbed a second time Bill fought
substitute Ted Hinton. Nevertheless it was Bill's biggest ever payday,
collecting £25 for his twelve round win. Johnny Walker's next aim
was to get Bill a match with George Rose the Bristol Wonderboy.
Rose had fought for the title the previous year and after Rose and his
manager Jack King had seen Billy beat Bert Hutchins at Eastwood

Open Air Show the fight with Rose was fixed for fifteen rounds. The fight was made for £100 with the winner receiving £60. Unfortunately before the action took place Walker died and as Billy had lost his backing the fight was off.

Disappointed he decided he was going to have a month or two back home but as he was coming up the North Road on his new motorcycle, he hit a car outside Retford. Injuries to his hands and feet meant his boxing career was over. A job was obtained at English Electric but this ran out after three years in 1934.

Being out of work in the thirties was no joke so Bill decided to make a ring comeback. It seemed as if he had never been away. During the year he had twenty fights and only lost one, that being on a cut eye. His victories included wins over Gunner Thompson, Charlie Bitmead, Johnny Bell, George Humphries and two wins over Sam Minto, the coloured American who had been in the ring with several champions on the continent. Fights were harder to come by in 1935, of his twelve matches four were lost including defeats by Irishman Billy Walsh and that great Midlands campaigner Len Wickwar, The same difficulties occurred in 1936 and his record for the year was fifteen contests with four defeats. He was knocked out in two rounds by Frenchman Tony Renaud, but beat the Smiling Kid at Edmonton and boxed a ten round draw with Irishman Danny Webb.

Fights were very spasmodic and Billy's last appearance was in 1939 when he beat Stan Stone at Rayleigh over eight rounds. During the next six years it was Army service, the only ring appearances being for fun. In quite a long career Bill Sedgwick surpassed 146 contests with only twenty-one defeats.

Hal Bairstow

The late 1930s saw the rise of a young Morton boy who became one of the most promising middleweights in the country. He was Harry Bairstow.

Young Harry's potential was spotted by local manager Harry Beckett, who looked after several youngsters including Paddy Quinlan and Ed Kelly. Beckett, who christened his prospect Hal had an outlet for his fighters at the *Elephant and Castle* in Knaresborough. Hal made his pro debut there stopping Neurel in three rounds. In his first ten fights, eight of them at Knaresborough, Hal won every one, eight being knockouts or a case of his opponent retiring. Two of his victories were on the same night. Hal had knocked out Bradford's Jack Beatty in the first round and was immediately challenged by

Hal Bairstow, backed by manager Harold Beckett.

Pudsey's Tug Wilson and Hal climbed into the ring for the second time to duly give Wilson the same one round knockout treatment. Seasoned campaigner Teddy Duffy with the experience of over 100 fights was expected to give the youngster his hardest fight to date, but he went the same way as the rest and was well beaten in three rounds. Manager Beckett won for himself a silver medal for having trained the largest number of successful boxers seen at Knaresborough in a year.

Well known sportsman Clarrie Jackson opened the 1938 season with promotion at the Keighley Baths Hall and Hal was given his first chance to appear in front of his own fans. Huddersfield's Tommy Kennedy was expected to give the youngster a good test and indeed after the first round when Kennedy landed good right hooks to the face and body, it looked as if Bairstow had his work cut out. But in the second round, Hal got in some accurate straight lefts, and after Kennedy had taken two counts, a right hand to the jaw finished it in the same round.

There was no stopping the Morton boy and in the next couple of months he fought three times at the Brunswick Stadium and twice at Pontefract Baths. His punching power produced three knockouts and two stoppages. The five fights, lasting a total of thirteen rounds. His record on 1 January 1939, read sixteen fights, sixteen wins all inside eight months and all bar one had finished well inside the distance. Hal's next match turned out to be his first defeat and what a contest it proved. Fighting at Brunswick against Rotherham's Jim Stuart he had his opponent down twelve times in the eight round contest. Despite giving away 7lb he struck with such power that Stuart took ten counts of eight in the last three rounds. But this was not convincing enough for the referee who gave the verdict to Stuart on points!

The defeat was soon shaken off for in Hal's next five contests four were won by knockouts, the other by stoppage. In March 1939 he took part in his first ten rounder and topped the bill at Pontefract against the much more experienced Sheffield boxer Matt Morgan who boasted of never being knocked out. The Morgan fight was good experience and despite tiring towards the finish Hal had done enough in the early rounds to take the decision. Several more victories including ones over Billy Smith of Huddersfield and Cyril Jackson of Manchester and Hal's record of twenty-five fights, twenty-four wins was as good as any boxer in the country.

The poster advertising Hal Bairstow's fight against Lancashire's new sensation Mick Egan, at the Brunswick Stadium, billed the contest as the severest test of Bairstow's career, and that is what it turned out to be. It was a setback when, for the first time in Hal's career, the referee had to intervene after six rounds to save him from further punishment. After being down for several counts, Bairstow had shown a remarkable degree of courage to get back into the fight and it was a big disappointment when the referee stopped it, as he was convinced the match was by no means over.

Worse was to follow when three weeks later at the same venue, the 8lb heavier former amateur champion Harry Hampston landed a knock out punch. It was sweet revenge for Hampston, for only three months earlier his seconds threw in the towel against Bairstow.

Matt Morgan who had given Hal one of his hardest fights was to be his next opponent at Keighley Gala. Morgan had to withdraw and was substituted by Jed Harland who had already been beaten by Hal. Harland fared no better than last time and fell to a third round knock out.

After fighting his entire career in the West Riding Hal made several appearances in the Northeast. He lost a very close points decision to Jim Laverick at Whitley Bay but bounced back with a quick knockout against Army champion Drummer Britt in the same hall a fortnight later. He then completed two victories in a week knocking out Bill Mounsey at Morecambe and stopping Jim Laverick at South Shields.

Hal's next appearance was at the famous Liverpool Stadium against veteran Birkenhead boxer Charlie Smith who was one of the leading welters in the north. Smith proved too much for the Morton fighter and Hal was beaten in two rounds.

Another match with Laverick was a big draw in the NorthEast and the pair met again at Middlesbrough and once again Hal's luck was out. His sheer aggression made the fight a thriller and Bairstow considered himself unlucky not to get a draw. Hal's popularity in the Northeast saw him complete a further four matches in the area during which he knocked out Billy Lawrence in four rounds, fought two thrilling contests with Middlesborough's Jim Teesdale, finishing one each and took part in a fourth match with Laverick at Newcastle. Again the fight was accepted as a substitute but this time Laverick got the clearest result of their meetings when the referee stopped it after eight rounds.

By this time Hal was in the services and appearances became less frequent. On his resumption he never boxed with the same consistency that had been the feature of his early career. In nine fights he only won once and after Bruce Woodcock's brother, Billy Carrol, had completed two victories over him he decided to hang up his gloves. His record of fifty contests in which he won thirty-two, the majority by knockout, was a lot less impressive than it looked at the half-way stage when he had only been beaten once.

The prowess of his punching power had seen few equals in Keighley and although he didn't receive the popularity of some of the earlier locals mainly due to the fact that when he was at his height people were concerned with the War, he deservedly takes his place among the prominent boxers to come from the area.

CHAPTER 15

Leeds Venues and Promotions

The Early Days

The demise of the bare fist fight and the introduction of the Queensberry Rules saw the start of the gymnasium boxing club era and by the 1890s came the formation of schools of combat, with boxing included in the programme. Gymnasium clubs run by ex-boxers in converted premises quickly sprang up and it was a natural extension to run tournaments as a means of making the gym viable. The sport was still restricted by the authorities who were not convinced that brutality and money wrangles, which had hounded the fight game's early history, would not disappear now that the sport had moved inside.

During 1892 boxing shows were run at a stable in Briggate featuring Leeds boxers Tom Moran and John Coyne. A famous match took place there that was still fresh in an eye witnesses account many years later. Parrott of Doncaster gave a boxing lesson to a Leeds opponent, who was four stones heavier! Publicity of the wrong kind ensued following a contest that took place at Tommy Molloy's gymnasium in the city during 1894. The fight was a grudge match between Willie Morn and Fred White, both of Leeds and the latter, in particular, had built up quite a name locally in the boxing world. Fought before an unruly crowd, the two men had only been fighting for two minutes when the referee had to enter the ring to part them. The boxers became so agitated that near the end of the second round, White deliberately threw Morn. The referee entered the ring again and gave the decision to Morn on a foul, whereupon White then tried to assault the referee. White's seconds entered the ring in the same frame of mind followed by Molloy and some of the other boxers on the bill who, in trying to cool matters, only added to the confusion. The whole affair ended in a riot and certainly not the kind of publicity the people trying to establish boxing in the town needed.

By 1900 the Leeds County Athletic Club in Harrison Street was holding regular boxing shows. The most popular boxer to appear at the club was Sticker Atkinson from Bradford. Sticker, the eight stone champion of Yorkshire, a title he had won in front of 2,000 people at St George's Hall, won the Leeds crowd over after his contest with T Ganley of Birmingham when he arose from the canvas about thirty times to stop Ganley in the later rounds. After the club closed for a while and was re-opened by a famous name in Leeds boxing, Harry Dorsey, there was only one bill topper Harry wanted and Atkinson duly obliged with a creditable thirteen round win over Brady for the entire gate receipts.

The other Leeds main venue in 1903 was the Jewish Athletic Club in Sheepscar Street: A great favourite at Sheepscar Street was the Leeds Irish Champion, Kid Saxby, who a few years later had his hands injured by revolver shots when trying to cover his face. This was a sequel to a series of incidents after a fight at a Jewish Club.

The Boxing Boom
Any available premises such as unused warehouses were quickly adapted as training centres. Most of them had Sunday training sessions followed by tournaments as many as possible would be squeezed into the room and because it was illegal to charge admissions on Sundays a silver collection would be taken. Other examples in Leeds were the early venue 'underneath the arches' which was down the side of the Queens Hotel. Other examples were Dobby Mills at Kirkstall, Mick Sunderland's 'threepenny shop', Tommy Oates' gym in Holbeck and Bakers in St Luke's Street.

Champion, Harry Mason started his career in Foster Thompson's gymnasium, which was in an attic above a garage in Newcastle Street. As the boom developed, bigger premises were needed and promoters like Arthur Heslop, Percy Green, the Fox's and later Jim Windsor began to bring some big names to Leeds. The main venue in Leeds in the twenties was the Leeds National Sporting Club in Templar Street. The promoter was Arthur Heslop who had run earlier shows in Leeds and was involved with promotions at the Ideal Skating Rink, Harrogate and the Windsor Baths in Bradford. Novices were invited to attend the gym sessions and to enter the mid week open competitions with a chance of obtaining a place on the regular Sunday afternoon bill. To accommodate big names Heslop booked Leeds Town Hall, but obviously boxers of the top calibre meant a dearer admission charge. Equally popular were the bills composed of locals with whom the supporters could have an affinity. The shows, which offered six fights for seven pence, gave a dozen or so lads their chance, This was the era of unemployment and depression, the age of the 'hungry fighter'. More and more capable men were turning to

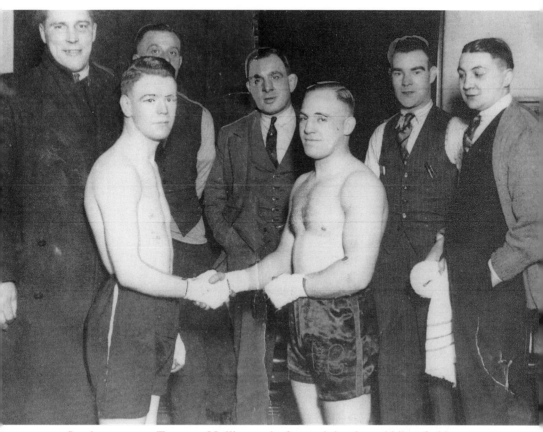

Leeds manager **Tommy Mallinson** is featured in the middle of this photograph. The two boxers are, on the left - **Jack Manley**, Bradford, and on the right - **George Gledhill**, Halifax.

boxing.

In the early 1930s two other famous names in Leeds boxing promotion staged tournaments at Brunswick stadium, Percy Fox brother of champion Joe, and Jack Green. The Leeds public had several choices, another alternative being the Leeds Ring in Marshall Street, which was run by Tommy Oates with Joe Carter his manager and matchmaker.

The two managers in Leeds during the sport's heydays were Tommy Mallinson and Prof. Lou Marks. Mallinson, an ex-boxer from Widnes, had fought in America in his younger days, and during his days at Newcastle Street, under Benny Fox's supervision, scores of fighters passed through his hands.

One of the greatest fighters to step into a ring in Leeds was Benny Lynch. The story of Benny Lynch, the World flyweight from the Gorbals, is one of the saddest in boxing history. Within eight years of winning the World title, Lynch was dead. Destroyed by drink and rough living. There was special interest in Lynch's appearance in Leeds. His opponent, Batley's Len Hampston, had experienced a controversial result in their previous meeting. Hampston was on the verge of beating Lynch until a second interfered with the fight and the referee stopped it on a disqualification. This time Lynch showed his class and Hampston was beaten in seven rounds. Jim Windsor sadly recalled Lynch visiting his club only a few days before his death. The Scot was down and out with his health badly impaired.

As the 1930s came to an end the boxing boom, which had pre-occupied the period, was fading and the only boxing shows to be held during the period were fund raising efforts for contributing towards the War. When boxing was revived after the War, the number of promotions were vastly reduced. The sport's heydays were over leaving behind it some of boxing's fondest memories.

Jim Windsor

Jim Windsor started promoting in the city in 1929. After a spell as manager for the 'Greens' at Brunswick Stadium, Windsor opened his own premises at the Windsor Stadium in Kirkstall Road. Formerly a picture house, the venue was eventually eclipsed when the area was

A promotion card for **Jim Windsor** - notice the title.

Television Series featuring

JIM WINDSOR of Leeds

CHAIRMAN AND MANAGING DIRECTOR OF
WINDSORS (SPORTING INVESTMENTS) LTD

AN AUTHORITY ON ALL SPORTS

Featured in Granada Television's

"NIGHTFALL" also

"ODDS-ON OUTSIDER" (This England series)

Featured in B.B.C's
MAY, 1974 SERIES
"WHO WANTS TO BE
A MILLIONAIRE?"

YOURS ON ALL SPORTS CHANNELS

World wrestling champion **Douglas Clark** whom Windsor promoted in a world title bout that sttracted 15,000 people.

demolished. Windsor gave many of the prominent Leeds boys their first chances. He ran a midweek cheap show, which was over in half an hour. He thought he would be finished for not giving value for money but the following week the hall was packed to the door. Word had gone round you could see six knockouts for sixpence. He introduced professional boxing at Armley Baths in the 1930s as well as running shows at Batley Carr and Ossett Town Hall.

Windsor was also one of the first promoters to introduce American-style all in wrestling. Many wrestlers were in fact rugby league men from Leeds and Bramley. Probably the largest crowd to see a wrestling bout in the country, 15,000 gathered to see rugby player, Duggie Clark, win the world title against Belgian Jersmen at Headingley. Brunswick promotions handled the return at Clark's homeground at Fartown the following week when Clark won in three rounds.

Windsor's last promotion in Leeds was between Freddie Mills and Leeds policeman Al Robinson in a heavyweight bout at Elland Road in 1943 as part of the RAF benevolent fund, the open-air event was ruined by heavy rain. Although the ring had a pool of water in the middle, the fight took place. Mills finishing the farce with a second round knock out. Boxing promotions were seriously curtailed when a heavy tax on turnover was introduced so Windsor turned to managing. His best fighter was Wakefield's Johnny McGown, the Central Area light heavy champion of the early 1950s who reached as high as number three in the British ratings.

In 1947 Windsor went to America to try and bring Joe Louis to Leeds for an exhibition but the champion's visit was limited to Earls Court. A world heavyweight champion did appear in Leeds in exhibition, the lesser rated Floyd Patterson.

Post War
When things started to return to normal after the Second World War, the boxing boom, which had pre-occupied the thirties, was over. Small hall promotions in the provinces were practically killed off in one swoop by the Government with a $33^{1}/_{3}\%$ entertainment tax on the promoters profit returns, promotions had always been a precarious business and the promoters could not rely on the fickle boxing fans to pay the extra admission charge to ensure against a loss. The result was that the number of venues dropped from 800 to 200. The lack of venues, plus the fact that the hungry fighter who had fought in the hard days for peanuts, had become more affluent and did not need boxing to sustain him, and so the number of professional boxers was vastly reduced. By the 1950s boxing, as a spectator sport, went further into decline when the great British institution – televison – started to introduce boxing on the small screen. Television helped make Cassius Clay the greatest name in sport and it made Henry Cooper the most popular British boxer whether he deserved to be or not. The ever increasing boxers' fees needed to put on the big names which the punters had seen on television was well out of reach of the provincial promoter. He had to rely on the best of the local talent from his area. The lack of big names to draw an audience and the preferences of the fan to become an armchair spectator was the final death knell in the provinces. The

death of the small hall promoter saw the return of the members clubs, which owed their association to the original National Sporting Club, which had dominated boxing prior to the First World War. The Sporting Club which had boxing as part of a night's entertainment and whose members threw more money into the ring than many old professionals earned for fighting while perhaps being out of reach of the ordinary working man ensured boxing's future.

In Leeds, Jack Green and then later his son Arthur, kept boxing alive in the city by holding an annual boxing tournament at the Town Hall. Held as part of the Leeds Jewish Sportsmen's charity effort, without the support of its patrons the tournament would not have been able to run so successfully for years. The annual show was instrumental in bringing to Leeds several champions in the making. Who can forget Hogan Kid Bassey, the Liverpool based Nigerian, who became world featherweight champion in 1957? His 1952 clash with Belgian Pierre Casseyms in which he was narrowly defeated was one of the best fights ever seen at the Town Hall. Bassey never forgot that Leeds defeat and the first thing he did after winning the world title was to hold a return at Liverpool against the Belgian and reverse the decision. The Nigerian made a second memorable Leeds visit in 1954 when he beat another Belgian, Aime de Visch. Howard Winstrone, Ken Buchanan and Jim Watt, all world champions during their careers made early appearances at the Town Hall. Yorkshire lad Alan Richardson, ABA champion and Commonwealth Games bronze winner and future British champion made his professional debut in Leeds in the same ring in which he was crowned champion. Another popular boy, Wakefield's middleweight Syd Parkinson who did not realise his predicted potential after an excellent amateur record, was also given his first chance in Leeds.

Leeds third British title fight came in 1982 at the Leeds Astoria (the scene of several promotions around the time) when Tom Collins who boxed out of the city, made a successful defence of his recently won British light heavy title. The explosive punching of Henry Wharton took Leeds boxing into the 1990s. Henry won and retained his Commonwealth Super Middleweight title at Leeds Town Hall and on the same night Frank Grant shocked the boxing world by beating Herol Graham, Henry beat 'Fidel Castro' to take the British Title at Elland Road.

CHAPTER 16

Richard Dunn

Before 1975 Richard Dunn's career had been a series of ups and downs. Always good enough to be well ranked in the British heavyweight ratings, his form never quite reaching the consistency that made him a logical contender for a British title fight. At the crossroads of his career and suffering from the despair of getting nowhere in the sport, he made a phone call to veteran boxing manager George Biddles to ask him to arrange some sparring at his gym. That was the turning point, for the next full year would prove to be his Indian summer as he became British heavyweight champion, followed that by taking the European title and then crowned his career off by fighting for the richest prize in sport against a boxer rated by most boxing followers as the greatest ever, Muhammed Ali.

Born at St James' Hospital in Leeds in 1945 not knowing his father, who was killed in the war, young Richard was brought up in Bramley before eventually moving to Bradford. The boxing career started when he was just short of twenty when as a paratrooper at Thornbury

Richard Dunn.

Barracks (on the road between Bradford and Leeds) he won a regiment tournament which saw him invited to train at Halifax Star Amateur Boxing Club under the tuition of former pro and club founder Bob Ennis. Before boxing became his serious sport, Richard had played amateur rugby league for a club in Halifax where his robust forward play as either prop or loose forward had seen him turn down offers from Huddersfield, Halifax, Oldham and Bradford Northern.

Reaching the ABA semi-finals three years running, Dunn became an England international and in his debut against Ireland he knocked out a future British champion in Danny McAlinden. Eventually becoming disillusioned with the amateur scene after a southern boxer named Harris whom he'd beaten got the England vest before him against Scotland; the Bradford based southpaw decided to become a Professional. Three years before he joined the paid ranks in 1969 when he signed for Retford manager, Ken Richardson, Richard had married into a boxing family. His wife Janet was the sister of the two Devanney boys, Jimmy and Lawrence, and his father-in-law Jimmy Devanney senior became his trainer. Dunn left his job with the Yorkshire Electricity Board to move onto a building site. His family moved into a corporation house at Buttershaw before eventually when the money started to come in, he was able to buy and do up a house in Undercliffe.

Richard Dunn's early pro appearances were in three round knock out tournaments. On the same night he had his first paid win in July 1969 (a three round points win over Del Phillips). Danny McAlinden gained revenge for his international defeat by completing a one round knockout against Richard. After two quick wins over Jack Coates in Manchester and Nottingham, Dunn won a November tournament in Bedford, where one of his victims was his old amateur rival Billy Aird from Liverpool.

For his first fight in Yorkshire Dunn was matched with Welshman Dennis Avoth at Leeds Town Hall. When it was learnt that Avoth's car had broken down whilst travelling north, Jamaican born Bradford light heavyweight Lloyd Walford climbed into the ring. Conceding two stone Walford, to say he had taken the fight as a last minute substitute, didn't let the crowd down, though he could not prevent Dunn gaining a six round points verdict.

There was upset in Dunn's first fight in 1970 when the scouser Billy Aird finally got the better of the Bradford bricklayer. Richard was fuming. He considered he had beaten Aird and the referee had got it wrong. Before the year was out Aird and Dunn met again for the vacant Central Area heavyweight title. Sandwiched in-between

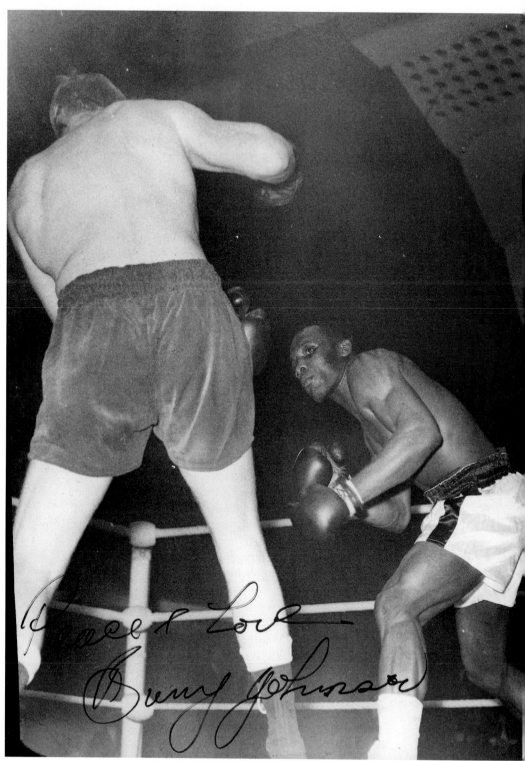

Richard Dunn and **Bunny Johnson**.

the Aird fights Dunn took his record to ten wins out of twelve with two victories over Obie Hepburn of Manchester and a points win over Billy Wynter at Bedford. The two rivals had met six times, Dunn had won all four amateur contests and the first three round pro meeting with Aird recording the disputed decision in the pair's last meeting. The crunch match turned out very disappointing for Dunn and his followers. Despite training harder than he had ever trained before for a fight, he never found his rhythm. Richard looked to have laid the foundations for a points win until Aird opened up in the sixth. The Yorkshireman had not the steam to stay with him, as Aird showing his first real aggression in the fight put Dunn down three times in the same round to take the title.

There was further disaster two months later when St Lucia's George Dulaire whom Richard had beaten earlier clashed heads with Dunn in the first round at Bedford. The eye injury, which needed five, stitches forcing a first round defeat when Dunn had to retire.

The two successive defeats were put in the shade when Dunn met Dennis Forbes a fortnight before Christmas. The Jamaican lasted just fifty-five seconds. Richard's solid left putting him down for counts of six and nine before delivering the knock out punch. There would be other one rounders but none as quick as that.

Dunn's first fight of 1971 was a bout he took as a last minute substitute for Dennis Avoth the Welsh heavyweight at the National Sporting Club. Newcastle's Brian Jowitt had won his last four matches but found he couldn't cope with Richard's aggression and the Bradford boxer was a clear points winner. Birmingham based Jamaican Bunny Johnson, then along with Jack Bodell, part of George Biddles' stable was really a light heavyweight who, like Bradford's Jamaican Lloyd Walford campaigned as a heavyweight because fights were difficult to get at the lower weight and at times it was more lucrative to be a heavyweight, was Richard Dunn's next victim at Wolverhampton. With Johnson's record showing only four defeats from twenty-six, a World ranking of forty, a British rating of four behind Joe Bugner, Jack Bodell and Carl Gizzi and having won eight fights on the run including a win over Dick Hall then only one of two men to have beaten Joe Bugner, it was easily Dunn's best win to date and a result that brought him a big step forward. Opinion was that Johnson had underestimated the sandy haired bricklayer who did well, particularly in the third when Johnson's left looked like it might have Dunn in trouble.

A third successive points win came when the Harlesdon based Jamaican Denis Forbes did better in his second meeting with Dunn than when the couple met six months earlier. Forbes erasing the memory of his fifty-five second embarrassment but still comfortably beaten in eight rounds. The twenty-six year old bricklayer moved up to number four himself in the ratings when he ended Carl Gizzi's chance of another title shot. The experienced Welshman had fought Jack Bodell for the crown two years earlier and had sparred with Richard before the fight. After Dunn's eight round points win (his fourth such result in succession) at the Midland Sporting Club, Solihull, Gizzi said afterwards that his Yorkshire opponent had deserved to win and he had obviously learnt more than he thought from their sparring sessions. Referee Roland Dakin had given Gizzi only two rounds out of the eight with Dunn, who was in total command throughout, having his best round in seven when Gizzi did well to survive with a bloodied nose. The week after with Richard now in the frame for a British title fight, the home boxing scene was shocked by southpaw Jack Bodell regaining the heavyweight champion over holder Joe Bugner. The thirty-one year-old Swadlincote (Derbyshire) farmer was like Richard Dunn, he had hauled himself up from the bootlaces to reach the top in boxing without unlimited financial resources behind him.

Nicknamed the Dunstable destroyer, Cliff Fields had won twelve out of fifteen when he was matched with Dunn in front of a packed 3,300 crowd at the Nottingham Ice Rink. The crowd had come to see Joe Bugner tackle the American, Larry Middleton. It was after the fans had become restless watching Joe outpoint his little known opponent over ten tedious rounds that Dunn warmed up the proceedings by forcing the referee to stop Fields in four rounds. A severe two inch gash above Fields eye giving the man in the middle no alternative. A euphoric Dunn stating his challenge from the ring to Bugner (or Joe Hamburger as he sometimes liked to call him) anytime, anywhere.

In December 1971, for the first time since Fred Ashton's promotions at the Windsor Hall Baths in the early 1950s professional boxing returned to Bradford with the revival of boxing in the city following the current trend in the sport, the formation of a sporting club. Sometimes criticised for taking the sport away from the working man, the formation of this type of members club had helped preserve boxing in the provinces. After the first venture at the Midland Hotel, the successful promoter Alan Jubb was promising Richard Dunn would be his next top of the bill in February 1972. The night after that statement Richard Dunn's title hopes were in tatters when the Leicester based Antiguan Rocky Campbell took him out in the first round of a scheduled eight rounder. There was nothing to suggest what would happen in a fight Dunn had no need to take, but took to keep busy. A big swinging right hander put Dunn down for a seven count. Frantic shouting by manager Ken Richardson saw Richard on his feet. The Buttershaw fighter tried to push Campbell away until the bell sounded only for Campbell to release a right uppercut, which saw Dunn fail to beat the second count. After his first round win in only two minutes, fifty-two seconds Campbell issued a challenge to McAlinden who had a controversial win over Chuck Oliviera on the same bill.

For a long time even up into the nineties when Frank Bruno mania was about and particularly in the heavyweight range a succession of Americans came over to this country to fight our leading men. Because America has dominated world boxing history, there seemed to be the fascination that because a boxer was an American he was top class. For a while it seemed like every time one of our heavyweights i.e. Bruce Woodcock, Henry Cooper and Brian London tried to make a move onto the world's boxing stage he was toppled by a 'Yank'. Sometimes the Americans who arrived in this country were name fighters with decent fight records and sometimes it was hard to even find a reference in America. It was not unknown for fighters to have invented bogus records to help put bottoms on seats. Some just came for the money and were not that bothered that they were being used as fodder to build up a British boxer's records and reputations. Joe Bugner fought one or two dubious ring men as did Bruno in his climb up the ladder and in his career against stateside boxers Richard Dunn came across a couple who were not up to scratch.

Richard's first American opponent Ron Oliver helped him get over the Campbell defeat as Dunn recorded a one round win at the World Sporting Club in London. A short but powerful left hook had felled the twenty-two year old former Golden Gloves champion from Brooklyn, who in his first year as a pro had won three out of four in America. Dickie later described the punch as like the one he did McAlinden with when he beat him as an amateur.

After the show had been switched from Sheffield by matchmaker Tommy Miller, Dunn made his first Bradford appearance at The Midland the following month in an all Yorkshire affair against Hull's Roger Tighe. Commonwealth gold medallist at light heavyweight Tighe had recently stopped Welsh champion Eddie Avoth and was the heavier at fifteen stone. In a £5.50 a ticket dinner show, Richard went ten rounds for the first time to record a points win that was so convincing that Tighe was not credited with one round. Dunn's forceful right hand repeatedly finding its way through Tighe's guard in what was Richard's eighth win in nine outings. A jubilant Jubb was talking about Dunn now meeting Bugner, Bodell or McAlinden in an open-air tournament at Odsal Stadium. Richardson was involved in talks with Jack Solomons, for the legendary promoter was working with Danny McAlinden and before Richard stepped into the ring six months later 'Dangerous Danny' had taken the British title from Jack Bodell in a two round roughhouse more akin to a bar room brawl in the wild west.

Dunn's ring return in October 1972 saw him produce a 'demolition job' on French Canadian Larry Renaud. The twenty-nine year old Montreal based boxer had reportedly won twenty-six out of twenty-nine on the other side of the Atlantic and had beaten Bill Drover who was known in England but was much lighter than Richard and couldn't bridge the disadvantage. A barrage of punches finishing him in one minute, forty-five seconds of the fight. Richard was now a regular at the WSC and his next American opponent was the brother of boxing legend Floyd Patterson. Ray, like his brother, was from Brooklyn but had quit the States to become a naturalised Swede. He also fought in the same 'peek a boo' style as Floyd. McAlinden had struggled to draw with him two years earlier whilst Bugner had beaten him but the decision got a hostile reception. Patterson posed problems as Dunn took a long time as the Yorkshireman seemed to let his concentration wander and it was felt if Patterson had been a stronger puncher, Dunn might have been in trouble. Patterson was a stone heavier than he had been in the summer and was only five pounds lighter than Richard was and as a consequence Dunn couldn't push him around the ring as he often did with lighter opponents. Richard took the verdict but there was only half a point in it.

Dunn was at the club again two months later for his first fight of 1973. Boxing at fifteen stone for the first time Dunn recorded a comfortable win over the 6ft 5in Roy Williams from Philadelphia. The following month Richard met another American this time at Wolverhampton, and the occasion proved farcical. Dunn's opponent was one of Ali's former sparring partners from the Angelo Dundee camp, Russell Brassell. The problems started in round one when Dickie tested the American with a range of hefty blows. Brassell complained bitterly that Dunn had hit him low in the kidneys and at the back of his head. Despite warnings from the referee Frank Parks, Brassell turned his back and refused to fight. Parks had no alternative but to bring the farce to an end and the American was disqualified leaving Dunn appealing to the 2,000 strong crowd with his hands and question 'what else could he have done?' Brassell had supposedly won seventeen out of twenty-two fights but no one could see how. Richardson announced his man would fight one more American before he met old rival Billy Aird in an eliminator for the British heavyweight title. The following day the Boxing Board of Control announced that they were holding Brassell's £450 purse. Also that day Dunn's rival Joe Bugner went twelve rounds with Ali and earned press praise for doing so. Ali made two statements after the fight. He said he would retire in two years (he fought until 1980) and that Bugner would become a future World title. (He was eventually proved right when on his umpteenth comeback at almost fifty, Bugner won one of the obscure versions of the World title).

George Foreman and an impressed Jack Solomons were in the audience when Richard completed his fourth win over an American. John Griffin a twenty-nine year old railroad worker from Cleveland, Ohio was sent to the canvas fifty-five seconds into round three by a Dunn left hook after the 21lbs lighter rated light heavyweight had annoyed the Bradford boxer by refusing to shake hands at the weigh in and trying to rely on flashy feints to get himself out of trouble.

Now it was time to meet Aird in the eliminator (the winner was to meet the winner of the Bunny Johnson versus the unbeaten Reading heavyweight Les Stevens clash in a final eliminator). This time the ringside guest was Ken Norton the man who had achieved fame for breaking Ali's jaw. The pairing produced ten gruelling rounds, with Dickie unable to nail Aird but still finishing a worthy points winner. Dunn's only real worry being a clash of heads, which after some good corner work didn't make any difference. Aird, who also lost his Central Area title in the fight, talked of retiring but he was still on the scene when Richard called it a day a few years later.

Solomons latest American import was 'a couple of tyres round his middle' eighteen stone Larry Belifuss. The twenty-six year old Wisconsin mechanic's claim to fame was that he had a decision over Morrie Jackson who had beaten McAlinden. Belifuss had arrived expecting to fight 'Dangerous Danny', but when McAlinden pulled out and Dunn's opponent Eddie Brooks from Milwaukee didn't arrive, Belifuss got in the ring with the Bradford man. After Dunn's first flurry of punches the ending looked obvious. Belifuss lasted until round four where his roly-poly frame hit the deck with a thud. It was Richard's seventh victory over a stateside boxer in eighteen months. Richardson was pleased for his other heavyweight, John Celebanksi, won on the same bill in a revenge match against Ralph Green of Durham.

Bunny Johnson had won the other eliminator against Stevens and

Johnson and Dunn met again on a Gus Demmy promotion at Belle Vue Manchester. McAlinden was to have topped the bill, but when he pulled out because a suitable opponent couldn't be found, the fight was postponed for a few days. Dunn was hoping to be the first Yorkshireman since Bruce Woodcock twenty-three years earlier to fight for the British heavyweight title. It was a great scrap but the wrong result for the coaches of fans who had travelled over the Pennines. Johnson conceded 21lbs but it did not stop him from putting Dunn down in both the fifth and seventh rounds. Recovering Dunn brought the crowd to its feet when he put Johnson down in the eighth but it was Dunn who was laid horizontal and counted out as Johnson snatched victory from defeat in round ten. Afterwards Johnson's manager George Francis admitted if it had not been a fight with something at stake he would have pulled his fighter out with his badly cut eye at the end of the eighth round.

Snazzily dressed in a leopardskin with long 'Joe Frazier' type shorts, Obie English was Richard Dunn's next American opponent. English, whose record was twelve wins from fourteen, did well to survive the early action as he almost buckled in the second round after Dunn had thrown three real punishing right handers. Though it was doubtful whether he had won a round, English survived until ten seconds short of the fight's ten round duration when the referee stopped him for the first time in his career. Dunn had bounced back in the best way but a cut above his left eye meant he had to cancel his next fight, which was to have been in Berlin against Bernard August in February 1974.

Dunn's next American adversary certainly was not an unknown. Jimmy Young was Joe Frazier's main sparring partner and during his career Jimmy would meet all the top 'Yanks' including Forman and Ali. Young was the first man from the States to beat Richard when the twenty-five year old, Philadelphia truck driver stopped Dunn in round eight. The ending was unexpected and it was thought Dunn was in front when referee, Sid Nathan, counted Dickie out whilst he was still on his feet. Dunn had risen from a knock down and was unsure of his bearings.

Dunn made his Germany trip two months later than planned but didn't fight August. He met the unknown Nigerian born Germany based Ngozika Ekwellum. The fight was very controversial and Richardson bitterly criticised the result as scandalous. In front of a crowd of 5,000 enthusiastic Germans at the Deutschland Halle, the sandy haired Yorkshireman looked set for victory when the referee counted him out on his feet in round seven of an eight round contest. After Ekwellum had been down three times in the fifth round and had taken two long counts in the sixth, Richard went in for the kill in round seven. The Nigerian caught him on the left temple with a right and Dunn went down on one knee for a count of three. Incredibly the referee carried on counting, as Dunn looked ready to carry on. Even the Germans at ringside looked embarrassed and it was not the first fight that had ended in that fashion at the venue. Chris Finnegan felt robbed when his opponent was carried out of the ring utterly exhausted and the referee had given the fight verdict a draw.

After his first European trip, Richard made a second when he met the burly Basque, Jose Urtain, in front of his own partisan crowd in Madrid. Twice European champion, Urtain still had plenty to offer, as Dunn found out via a jolting right in the first round. Urtain urged on by his supporters would not be denied and to his fans' delight he dropped and finished Dunn with a powerful right in round four. It was Richard's fourth stoppage defeat in his last five outings and it was time to take stock of his career. Taking a holiday in Minehead to have time to think about his next move, Richard broke his vacation to take a fight with Tim Wood, the Leicester light heavyweight. Grinding out a morale boosting points win, Dunn's stone and a half advantage was too big a handicap for Wood who would later return to the light heavy ranks and win the British title at that weight in 1976. It was a double celebration too for brother-in-law Jimmy Devanney was on the same bill and he repeated an earlier victory over Alan Hardiman from Hemel Hempstead.

The next fight for the Yorkshireman would be his last for Richardson for Dunn had made that famous call to George Biddles and 'the old silver fox' had agreed to watch Dunn in action against Neville Meade. Fifty years in boxing, George's claim to fame was his association with Hogan Kid Bassey who under George's wing won the World featherweight title in 1949. In later years Wally Swift and Jack Bodell were his champions. George not only had the eye for talent he was a great instiller of belief. Commonwealth medallist Meade, a twenty-five year old Jamaican truck driver who had won a search for a heavyweight contest for £2,000 organised by Jack Solomons strode out of his corner as if he meant real business. Inexperience was the key and Meade who would become British champion in the eighties retired in round five after taking a lot of heavy punishment.

Biddles' claims for Dunn: a chance in an eliminator were accepted and Richard was matched with an opponent he had a score to settle with, Rocky Campbell. Dunn's other ring rival Bunny Johnson had become British champion after beating Danny McAlinden. Campbell had dispatched Dunn in a round in their meeting four years earlier but like Richard his career hadn't really happened. The thirty-one year old Antiguan was known to fade later in fights and probably that was Dunn's best bet to try and contain him until the fight's middle rounds. Dunn, obviously out to make an impression on the man who had agreed to take over his managership, was tense and nervous. Campbell himself had been out of action for eight months since losing to Belgian Jean Pierre Coopmans and looked rusty. Nothing much happened until Dunn's fierce right cross had Campbell spinning at the end of the sixth. In the seventh Richard went for it and Campbell couldn't keep him off, with the referee being forced to stop the action because Campbell was unable to defend himself.

In his thirty-ninth fight and in his seventh year as a professional, Richard Dunn was fighting for his first British title. Thirty-one year old Dunn was Johnson's first defence and promoter Harry Levene had assured £10,000 for the winner and Levene was already talking to Belgian Coopman to fight the winner for the European title which had been vacated by Joe Bugner. Richard was seeing the fight as his last chance for the big time, and the Bradford scaffolder (he was a scaffolder as well as a brickie) had got himself fitter than he had been for a lot of fights. Dunn was the underdog with all the experts going for Johnson who went into the fight on the back of a four year, twenty-one fight undefeated run and a seventh in the World rating. Seventy-one year old Biddles had been Johnson's manager and his plan was for Richard to boss Johnson both physically and mentally from the start. Once Dunn was in front there was no way back for Johnson. Dunn's desire saw him if not the better boxer then the more determined. Taking the initiative in the middle of the fight Richard made his superior weight count. In the fifteen rounds which Dunn won by 4 1/2 points, Dunn won nine rounds whilst four were shared.

After the celebrations of becoming Bradford's first British champion had died down, Richard Dunn was out to create history for after only thirty-five days of being champion, Dunn was stepping into the ring for his first defence against former champion, the Coventry based Irishman, Danny McAlinden. If he won he would be on course to win an outright Lonsdale Belt in record time, but if Dunn lost he would be the shortest ever reigning British champion. 'Dangerous Danny' had won twenty-seven out of his thirty-four fights and the message was out that the fight would be over in no time, especially as their other two meetings hadn't reached the end of the second round. Terry Lawless, Danny's trainer, warned fans not to drop their programmes or they might miss the fight whilst Jimmy Devanney said 'Make sure you're in your seats in time'. Dunn was now feeling the price of fame that went with being the British heavyweight champion. He received £10,000 for his first defence and never seemed to be off local television and the press. The one person who did miss the fight was Richard's wife Janet who went out of the stadium to see to one of her children and missed the four-minute action. Not only had his explosive victory brought him a European title fight, the news was out that World champion Muhammad Ali wanted to defend his title in Europe in early 1976 and after his quick rise up the boxing ranks Richard Dunn was very much in the frame to meet him.

For his last fight of 1975, London promoter Mike Barrett had lined Dickie up to fight American scrapper Ron Stander who had fought Joe Frazier for the title in 1972, with the papers full of speculative opponents everyday, a concrete offer did come from Don King for Richard to fight Frazier in the Bahamas. Biddles had no hesitation in not taking the fight. He wanted the European title first which would obviously give the manager more bargaining power. The Stander fight did not materialise; instead Dunn fought the unheard of in England Terry Kreuger, the supposed Texan KO King. According to his manager Jim Parks, the 6ft 3in Texan had won thirty-two out of forty-one fights. Five of his opponents had finished up with broken jaws and Parks claimed Kreuger's twelve second flattening of Kammie Abbejar of West Africa in San Antonio three years earlier, was the fastest knock out ever achieved by a heavyweight. (Jack Dempsey put paid to Fred Fulton in eleven seconds in 1917, which like Kreuger's feat includes the ten second count). Booing and jeering started from the second round and it was obvious that yet another American wasn't up to the task. Dunn's left finished it in the third, not that the result was ever in doubt. While it was good to see his man stay on course for a European title, Biddles had hoped for a better work out for Richard. After a fight with Ernie Shavers the man with the reputation of having the best one punch hit in boxing was cancelled when Dunn developed flu during February, Dunn contested the European heavyweight title in April 1976. The title having become vacant when Joe Bugner had opted to go for World honours. Richard as expected was matched with the Belgian Jean Pierre Coopman but when the Belgian dropped out because he too was chasing a World title fight there was difficulty in selecting Dunn a suitable opponent. Coopman, Bugner and the Spaniards Alfredo Evangelista and Jose Urtain and even Billy Aird were unavailable for one reason or another and Dunn was matched with the German Bernd August whom he should have fought once before in Berlin.

August was not the draw the Royal Albert Hall pundits expected but at least there was not the jeering that had accompanied Richard's last fight there. August, the 6ft 7in German had won twenty-one fights out of twenty-four (he had drawn with Aird and lost to Coopman) had proclaimed that Dunn had a glass jaw in the fight build up. It was August who was found to be vulnerable as Dunn buckled his knees in the opening round. August had no answer as Dunn closed his left eye and it was a surprise when the German wasn't retired by his seconds at the end of round two. The referee finished it in the third and when a crown was put on Richard's head the crowd went ecstatic. Now the scene was set for the fight that had already been provisionally arranged, the fight that would set Richard Dunn up for life and by far the biggest fight of his career. Becoming European champion made Dunn a national celebrity and amongst the many accolades was the honour of being a featured personality on 'This is Your Life'. The fight with Ali was fixed for Munich and took place a month after his European triumph. The date, 25 May 1976, was a couple of weeks over a year since the Campbell fight, a year in which he had won a title eliminator, the British title, The European title and now he was meeting a living legend, a man who had every right to call himself the greatest for the ultimate prize in sport.

Richard did his training for the fight in the Midlands before leaving for Germany. Neville Meade and Eddie Fenton (a long time Dunn sparring partner) went over to help his training and after Richard had settled in his German camp, Ali and his forty strong contingent arrived and then the pre-fight banter to sell tickets between the two camps started. Odds were 14-1 on a Dunn victory and there was an outcry over the heavy price of tickets, which kept the crowd down to less than expected. The champion was expected to clear three quarters of a million whilst Richard's share was £100,000. Forty million were expected to watch on close circuit television including a party at the Bradford Executive Club.

Although there was no fairytale ending to the rags to riches story, Richard Dunn won many admirers with his brave performance when showing remarkable gameness he gave Ali all he knew against a man who was back to his best. For three rounds there was nothing in it as Dunn caused surprises by carrying the fight to Ali even giving him problems. In the fourth round the champion cut loose with a right upper cut which put the Bradford man down. Coming straight back up Richard was forced to take the mandatory count by the German ref. Back into the fray Dunn met a champion intent to finish the job and Richard was down twice more before the end of the round. There was no surrender from the British champion, he motioned Ali

Richard Dunn, Bradford's British heavyweight champion attacks the world champion **Muhammad Ali** in the pairs world heavyweight titles clash in Munich, Germany, 1976. *Photo courtesy of Telegraph & Argus*

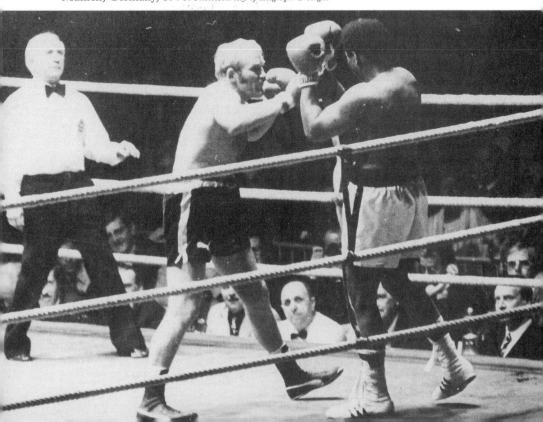

to come and get him. When Dunn hit the canvas again, the referee had no alternative but to curtail Dunn's challenge.

Richard was proud and overcome by the reception he received back in Bradford especially when it was announced that the new sports stadium that he had helped to build at the top of Manchester Road was to be named after him. Joe Bugner a severe critic of Richard's performance had annoyed television viewers by his comments. The former champion was persuaded to back up his remarks in the ring and because Dunn had always thought Bugner had avoided him in the pairs earlier days the scene was set for Bugner to end his retirement and challenge Richard for both his titles. The grudge match took place at Wembley and Dickie's quest for an outright Lonsdale Belt ended in disaster, the fight only lasting 134 seconds. Hitting with power and aggression he never showed normally Bugner had backed up his own statements.

Job done, Bugner retired again (as he frequently did during his career) and it was a year later before Richard entered the ring for his last fight which took place in Ellis Park in the Transvaal at a venue 5,600 feet above sea level. There were two white South Africans making noises in the world heavyweight scene, Gerry Coetzee and Kallie Knoetze. Richard fought the latter who had only two defeats on his record one of which was by his rival Coetzee. Knoetze had won his last four fights and although the financial reward was worth the trip to Johannesburg, Dunn was annoyed that the sparring partners provided by the Africans were two inexperienced seventeen-year-olds, and an eighteen stone heavyweight. Richard was stopped in the fifth when it was thought he would have enough in the later rounds to have beaten the South African champion.

Though there was still the ambition of a Lonsdale Belt and there was talk of Richard meeting his old rival Billy Aird for the title which was vacant again, Richard called it a day ending the sport a much richer man than he could have ever possibly dreamed a couple of years earlier. After his ring retirement Richard moved to Scarborough and unluckily things didn't work out well for him when he badly injured his legs after an accidental fall. In more recent years he has returned to Bradford to organise large car boot sales.

Though he had his critics by being the right man at the right time he put the area on the boxing map after it had spent many years in the doldrums.

CHAPTER 17

Tom Collins

F rom the minute he walked into his gym in 1976 and dipped his shoulder to throw a punch at a hanging bag, boxing manager Trevor Callighan, who had come to the fore in the manager stakes with the success of Fitzwilliam featherweight Alan Richardson, knew the strapping 5ft 6in Caracoa (Dutch West Indies) born twenty year old from Leeds Tom Collins had the credentials to make it in the world of professional boxing. With his early career perhaps more famous for a series of clashes with the boxing legend Dennis Andries who became a big hit in the States at an age when the majority of boxers would have been retired for some time. Like his rival Dennis and good wine, Tom got better with age and after a decade in the sport and in the twilight of his career, he clinched a third British light heavyweight title, twice became European champion and fulfilled every boxers dream by fighting for a world title

Tom Collins.

The former Market District Boxing Club amateur made his professional debut as a light heavyweight early in 1977 at Birmingham and stopped Ginger McIntyre inside four rounds. Fighting mostly around the Midlands and despite the disadvantage of a sparse career in the unpaid ranks, Tom stayed unbeaten for his first six fights with his punching power particularly his 'right hand bomb' accounting for four inside the distance wins. Perhaps it was too big a fight too early, for in his next match, Tom fought in Oslo and was beaten by one time World title challenger Harald Skag in eight rounds in 1978. All his early success became undone when Karl Canwell stopped him in six rounds in his London debut and the man who was to be his biggest foe beat him twice at Southend in Tom's last fight of 1978 and his first of 1979. The fights with Andries

Tom Collins, the West Indian Leeds boxer who won the British light heavyweight title on three separate occasions.

were both hard fought affairs. The first defeat was on points, but in the second Tom was knocked out for the first time, a feeling he wouldn't experience for another six years. Sandwiched in between the Canwell fight and the first Andries match was the Leeds man's first one round win when Carlton Benoit was knocked out in Sheffield.

With his record standing at nine wins from thirteen, Tom was matched with Greg Evans for the vacant Central Area title for his first bout of 1980. The occasion was Collins first appearance in the West Riding and the West Indian only needed one round to demoralise Evans at the Bradford Sporting Club. Collins' bombs ensuring the devastated Evans took two counts. There was a second Scandinavian trip and Collins dropped another decision this time to Uganda's Mustapha Wasajja in Denmark. Early in the fight, Tom shook the Ugandan with a tasty right hander, which badly hurt him. Mustapha was forced to take a standing count before recovering to outpoint Collins. Wasajja later beat Dennis Andries in a 'real maul' and became a World title challenger.

The Evans win helped assure a title eliminator and Collins returned to the scene of his Central Area win and produced his best form yet as he reversed an earlier decision against a man who had been the first to stop him. Karl Canwell was beaten on points and along with his rival Andries, Tom was in line for a crack at the British light heavyweight champion Bunny Johnson. Andries had had a go at Johnson but had lost on points to the former British heavyweight champion. Tom and Dennis were set for their third encounter in a final eliminator at Stoke, but the fight never took place. A routine medical revealed a blood disorder and a hint of heart trouble. It was a worrying time, but specialists finally cleared Tom. When he was passed fit to resume a year on he was fighting Dennis for the British title, for Bunny Johnson had vacated because of his continued residence in Australia. The Bunny Johnson versus Andries fight received a lot of bad press. The referee had described it as 'The worst bout I have ever refereed or watched'. Harry Mullan, the then editor of *Boxing News* went further: 'It was a graceless and at times farcical affair with Andries offering the crudest challenge I have ever seen'. Harry reported. Bunny Johnson was said to have stated: 'I'd give up the crown rather than go through that again'. Although he certainly wasn't textbook and at times looked wild and clumsy, Andries was highly effective. An iron chin, a solid punch and excellent stamina made him a hard man to beat. Big Tom was much more the polished article and round one wins proved he was no mean puncher. The

Canwell fight, which was his only fight in 1981, was his improvement landmark. Answering doubts about his temperament by outboxing his rugged opponent despite suffering a cut early in the bout. The verdict was Collins had to keep Andries at bay, possibly frustrating him with his longer reach left jab. The fight was at Bloomsbury Crest Hotel where Callighan insisted his man was only a novice in their two earlier meetings. It proved a great night for Collins. He outclassed and outlasted the 'Hackney Spoiler' by a wide margin. All the pre-match speculation about Collins' stamina was unfounded as he wore Dennis down. Tom had never gone past ten rounds as he stole to the British title. Andries who went down in round fourteen and was saved by the bell couldn't do anything about the Leeds man's straight left jab. There was criticism in the press that Collins had not thrown a punch in the first six rounds. But the tactics had proved correct as Andries slowed up. Tom had taken over in the later rounds and following on from Richardson, Trevor Callighan had produced another British champion.

It was decided it was about time Leeds could witness its new champion and for Tom's first defence, Callighan fulfilled a promise when Collins fought at the old Leeds cinema, The Astoria, against challenger Trevor Cattouse. Tom's opponent had two draws and eight defeats from twenty-seven outings whilst the champion's record was six defeats from eighteen. The last time a title fight had been held in Leeds had been five years ago when Trevor's earlier champion Richardson had fought at the Town Hall. Upset by the criticism about his man from the last fight, Trevor defended him by insisting he fought the right sort of fight and when Collins' punching power saw Cattouse who was attempting to follow in the steps of his lightweight champion brother Ray fall in four rounds. Trevor was quick to point out he had fought the right sort of fight against an entirely different type of opponent. The performance had given his Leeds supporters something to shout about especially the way Tom had finished his challenger. Ray Clarke, the Boxing Control General Secretary, was at ringside and Callighan expressed a second defence quickly, for he was ambitious for his boxer to beat the six-month outright Lonsdale Belt record held by featherweight Pat Cowdell.

The record chance never materialised and it was ten months before Tom had the chance to win his outright Lonsdale Belt. Before his second defence, Collins made his third Scandinavian appearance and suffered his third setback there. There was a host of Africans through limited chances in their own country making a living in Europe with Denmark in particular taking its fair share. Ugandan

John Odhiambo was beaten in his first eleven fights and added to his record when he destroyed Tom in five rounds. Collins was overmatched and from as early as the second round the Ugandan was breaking through with telling punches. Tom was in trouble for a round or two before the referee belatedly ended it in the fifth when the British champion was floored twice. The second defence had to be put back a couple of times while Tom recovered from a hand injury and there had also been neck problems since his last Copenhagen experience. Leeds was robbed of a title fight between Tom and the local fighter, the Irishman Liam Coleman who lost an eliminator to the Jamaican born Birmingham based Antonio Harris after Coleman had beaten Harris in a fight only two months previous to the eliminator. Harris had not been knocked down but he had lost to other contenders like Keith Bristol and Trevor Cattouse. Tom treated the Solihull crowd to his right hand 'bolo punch', as Harris never really looked the part. The local man felt Collins thunderous right every round and by round six when the challenger was trapped on the ropes, the referee had seen enough. Callighan was disappointed that his outright Lonsdale Belt holder could not clinch a European fight. Long time champion, Dutchman Rudi Koopmans seemed to defend against everybody bar Collins. Finding it difficult to be a big attraction on the British circuit and work not always easy to come by, Tom travelled to New Zealand to beat their prospect, Alex Sua in a commonwealth eliminator and then to Trinidad where he dropped a close decision to Lesley Stewart who since he had returned home had developed into a World ranked fighter.

Meanwhile Dennis Andries wanted his title back and the Guyana born bruiser showed he meant business in his two eliminators when both Karl Canwell and Keith Bristol were knocked out in the fourth round. Andries had the hunger and Tom lost his title to his big rival making the series score 3-1 to the new champion. It wasn't a classic but not many of Andries fights were. Collins didn't show to form; though for some of the fight he did look on top. Andries punches or at least the ones that landed took away the advantage that Collins looked to have built. The last time the two had met, championships were fifteen rounds and now Collins had lost his title to the new twelve round title length. The only solace was that if Tom did lose, a return was agreed. It was found that the ring at the Lyceum Strand was only fourteen-foot square instead of sixteen. Collins had refused the bout then relented after Callighan had argued with promoter Greg Steene that if his man had lost there would be an immediate return. Steene had claimed the original ring had been stolen from a garage in Blackfriars. It was thirty year old Andries third time as British champion and the new champion and Steene kept their promise for a return for Tom had saved the show when he had every reason to quit at an undersize Boxing Board of Control ring. The fifth, and what would be the last, meeting between the two light heavyweights was again down south, this time at Watford. The Boxing News preview of the fight questioned Collins' desire and sometimes erratic behaviour, which had on occasions seen him lose interest during a fight. Tom had the punch but it needed something exceptional to penetrate Andries seemingly chin armour. The disappointment was all over Tom's face after the rematch when he learned he had lost a very close verdict by only half a point. Trevor called the decision dreadful and thought his man should have won. Opinion differed on the result but the one thing that was agreed was that it was a very close, tight fight. Criticised for losing the previous fight through lack of work, Collins had put in a much more determined performance but the half a point defeat meant he had to pick himself up again after three successive defeats, approaching thirty, Tom's career looked to be nearing an end. But in reality it was only half way through and the Leeds man would clock up another twenty-five fights before he called it a day.

Worse was to follow and Collins only won two of his next seven. His days of becoming a champion again looked distant when he was beaten by two of the contenders in his division in Alex Penarski and Andy Straughn. The Penarski win was only the Alfreton man's fifteenth win in thirty-eight fights and he had only won once in his seven fights prior to the fight. The Andy Straughn fight was an embarrassing thirty-six second affair at Halifax in his first Yorkshire appearance since the Cattouse fight three years earlier. The triple ABA champion softened Tom up with a left hook and finished him in the next attack. The up and coming hit man from Hitchin was only rated eighth in the division rankings. Despite the form lull there was no hint of retirement. Europe again played a part in his plans and Tom lost on points to Chisanda Mutti in West Germany, Ralf Rocchisiani in Frankfurt, drew with Pierre Kabassu the French based African in Forbach France and knocked out Yawe Davis in three rounds in San Reno, Italy.

For his first fight in 1986 he met the Cardiff based Jamaican Winston Burnett in his second Leeds appearance, in a Callighan promotion at the Town Hall. That win put Tom back in the British title frame for Burnett was expected to fight the winner of the Tom Moody versus Kenny Bristol eliminator. Despite taking the fight at twenty-four hours notice, Burnett went the full eight rounds but couldn't prevent Tom taking the verdict. In the States, Dennis Andries' style suited the American audience and the 'Hackney Spoiler' had found a new fame. He did return to defend against Kenny Bristol but soon returned to more lucrative fights across the water and in April he won the World WBC light heavyweight title when he beat J B Williamson in Edmonton. Dennis defended his new World crown and his British title when he stopped Tony Sibson the former British middleweight champion who had moved up to the higher division, in nine rounds. With big fights on the horizon Dennis then vacated his British title.

In December, Tom was beaten for the fifteenth time in thirty-five fights when he dropped a points decision to Alex Blanchard the current European champion in Arnhem, Holland. The fight had been a twelve round, non-title bout and although Blanchard had looked World class in the first few rounds, Collins who suffered a knock down in the ninth round, had seen enough to convince himself he could beat the Dutchman if they fought again. On the domestic front there was a chance to regain his British lightheavy title when he was matched with John Moody, a descendent of the famous Welsh boxing family of the 1930s for the vacant title at the Royal Albert Hall. A few days before Tom's battle with Moody, old foe Andries was blasted out by the 'hitman' Tommy Hearns who reduced Dennis to a novice. Though Andries showed all his usual guts he was sent to the ground seven times.

Moody's strength and aggression compared well with Collins' skills until the sixth round when a couple of head clashes saw Moody receive several warnings and Tom a hairline cut. From the eighth round Moody looked unsteady on his legs and when Tom unleashed his speciality big right hand thirty seconds into round ten, he had regained the British title in his 32nd year. Earlier in his career when he had held the British title and even in the years when he was a No. 1 challenger, a European title fight had never materialised. Now he had the credentials again and with Blanchard having met him recently and beaten him, fulfilling another ambition was a formality. Tom celebrated his eleventh year as a professional by becoming a European champion. Blanchard never knew what hit him. The twenty-five year old Dutchman had completed five defences and had drawn with Andries when they had met twenty-two months earlier. Despite the Dutchman's form a stunning punch knocked him out in round two and he was on his back for a minute. A month after the European championship win, Tony Wilson who had beaten

Warrington's Blaine Logsden succeeded Tom who had vacated his British title in quest of higher honours. The up and down career of Tom Collins had taken a new route and Callighan was talking to the new promoter, Messiah Frank Warren about the possibility of a World title fight for his man.

The Leeds veteran was in line for a shot at the World IBF title held by 'Prince' Charles Williams. The fight was set for Dublin in February 1988 and then moved to April and then the venue changed to Cork before it was cancelled because Williams had accepted a non-title fight in Paris. Like Tony Sibson, Mark Kaylor had moved up from middleweight to light heavyweight (three and a half years ago he had lost his British and European title to 'Sibbo') and the West Ham hero, who boxed in the 'Hammers' colours was Collins' first challenger for his new title. The action was at Wembley and the forecast, knowing Kaylor's style, was for a short fight. The affair produced a bloody battle, which ended when Kaylor's corner man, Terry Lawless threw in the towel because his man had nothing left in round nine. Tom had looked in trouble in the early rounds, but had dug deep to save his title.

The first stint as European champion ended in May 1998 when Tom lost on a cut eye decision to Pedro Van Raamsdank at Riverside Leisure Centre in Reading. For five rounds Tom had plodded at the 6ft 6in, twenty-seven year old Dutchman who had moved carefully around the ring poking out a pole of a left arm. Just when Tom was starting to catch him with some good shots in the sixth; the Dutchman split Collins skin near the eye with the first punch of round seven. The cut was bad enough for the doctor to be called in and twenty-two seconds into the round Tom had lost his title. Disappointed at the earlier non-event with Williams and though his days in the ring were starting to be numbered, Tom still hankered after a World title fight. He was rated number two by both the WBC and the WBA, and nine by the IBF and was thrilled that his old rival Dennis was still doing the business at the top of the light heavyweight range. Even though the score with Dennis was 4-1, Tom always fancied his chances against him and believed he was the better boxer. Earlier in 1989 Dennis had regained his WBC title becoming the first Briton for seventy years to regain a World title. Dennis was fighting the Canadian and former champion Dan Lalonde next and although Tom might have preferred Dennis, Trevor Callighan was hoping Lalonde would win and there would be a mega bucks fight for Tom in New York.

In March Collins challenged for the British title held by Tony

Wilson who had become champion after Tom had vacated after winning the title for a second time. The fight went ahead at the Riverside, scene of Tom's last fight. With Wilson only one blot on his seventeen fight record and going into the match on the strength of six successive wins including three title victories, the new champion was strongly fancied in some quarters against the six year older former champion. When Tom got going with his big right hook and found the target, Wilson's legs turned to jelly and after Collins had followed up the shot with a left, the referee intervened and only fifteen seconds into round two the Leeds man was British light heavyweight champion for the third time.

Andries second spell as World champion was over, Australian Jeff Harding had beaten Dennis in Atlantic City to become the 'darling' of the division and big time promoter Bob Arum had promised Harding a big unification fight against the WBA champion Virgil Hill. Tom wasn't considered fashionable for his challenge to Harding to take place in England. At times labelled a 'Jekyll and Hyde' fighter, the Leeds based thirty-four year old was arguably in the best shape and form of his career. After his win over Andries the ten year younger than Tom, Australian wanted to show his countrymen in Brisbane that the win in America was no fluke and he was a worthy champion. For Tom Collins the fight ended in a very bitter disappointment. After waiting twelve years for it to happen, Collins was forced to retire from his inter-round stool after only two rounds. The Australian gave him a torrent of abuse and the Aussie press labelled him a Pommie coward. Arum went to town calling Collins a disgrace and the Australian's wanted to hold Tom's pay. Tom had taken a blow in the throat and had developed breathing problems and rather than risk his health Tom pulled out. There had been a protifation of press comment about safety in boxing and did anyone seriously think that a man who had waited twelve years to achieve his lifetime's ambition and flown half way around the world for it to happen, would have ended it deliberately on a stool in between rounds. Obviously the incident took some living down but Tom was not the first to quit in a World title fight and he wouldn't be the last.

There was no better way to erase the memory of the Brisbane debacle than re-confirm your rating with another European title and that's exactly what Collins did in August 1980, when he travelled to the French Mediterranean coast and knocked out the champion in his own backyard. Frenchman Eric Nicoletta had taken the title of Dutchman Jan Lefeber and had defended successfully against

Belgian Jose Seys and the tall Dutchman who had taken the title off Tom, Pedro Van Raamsdank. The fight was at Cap D'Agde in a converted ring at an open air venue with almost a hundred percent backing for the home man. Tom's thirty fight more experience told as the adopted Yorkshireman paced himself before knocking the champion out in round nine with a stunning punch and looking far from finished at thirty-five. The same month Collins had won his European title back; Andries had gone to Australia and finished Harding in seven rounds in Melbourne to restore English pride. Soon after it was revealed that the now three times champion was in fact two years older than stated and had beaten Harding at 38. Tom was in with another challenge, but there was a big demand for a third meeting between Dennis and Harding in 1991 and obviously Andries' handlers were interested in that much more lucrative business.

The French promoter who had put on the fight in Cap D'Agde wanted Tom back to France for his next outing. The French wanted their man to contest Tom's title, but the EBU turned down the request. Pierre Frank Winterstein normally campaigned as a middleweight and he pinched the ten round fight by applying a 'cat and mouse' game. The decision was close with one judge giving the fight even. It was yet another trip to France a few days before Christmas 1990 for Collins' twelfth fight in Europe (his third title) and though he would campaign until 1993, the occasion would prove to be Tom's last ever win as a professional. Christophe Giraud's little experience of ten unbeaten fights was cruelly exposed by the champion who could better the Frenchman's number of fights in championship bouts. Giraud, who was a voluntary defence by Tom, failing to last past two rounds.

In the following year Tom made another unsuccessful attempt at a World crown (1995 was not a good year for British light heavyweights for Jeff Harding had taken Andries' title). It was Collins' 48th fight and Callighan helped assure the vacant WBO title came to Leeds. A World title fight, the first in the city, drew the response and a packed Leeds Town Hall helped to see their man crown his long career with a coveted World title. Twenty-five year old Leonzer Barber had only made twelve ring appearances, but that did not mean he had to be taken lightly. Dennis Andries issued a warning, for he knew Barber well from the Kronk Gym in Detroit, that Tom's opponent had the quickest hands of any boxer at his weight. And Dennis had not exaggerated as Barber started to dominate from the opening bell. Tom did get his right hand moving

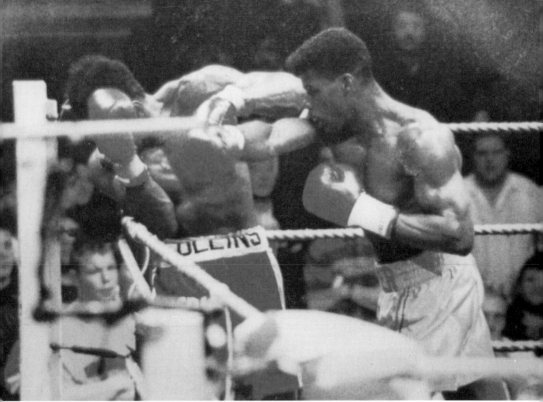

Tom Collins covers up in his world title fight with Leonzer Barber.

in the first round and Barber visually tottered for a second. The showing was brief as Barber took charge of the fight; a disturbing swelling on Tom's face came up like an orange on his forehead. The lump, which started growing after a first round clash had swollen to horrifying proportions by round six. There were echoes of Brisbane when Tom did not come out after round six. Callighan refused to let him continue and afterwards despite a feeling of humiliation Tom was adamant that his career was not over. German Graciano Rocchigiani took Tom's European title and it started to look like Collins certainly in the top flight had gone one fight too far. Confirmation came when he fought Johnny Nelson for his WBF cruiser title and was sent to the canvas three times in the first round.

Tom Collins had his detractors and was never box office a way a lot of other fighters were, the reason for his World travels where he fought the majority of his World title fights in his opponent's backyard. The tragedy will be if he is only remembered in time for losing two World title fights from his stool and not for his three times British light heavyweight championships, two European titles and a punching record which saw him stop nineteen out of twenty-six wins.

CHAPTER 18

John Doherty

Bradford finally had its first local born champion in January 1986 when Girlington featherweight John Doherty, after becoming at the same time the first Bradford man to contest a British Boxing Board title fight, won the vacant super featherweight title in his 27th professional fight and before his career terminated in the early 1990s John Doherty would become British champion a record three times.

Tommy Miller and Trevor Callighan were the main boxing managers in the West Riding in the 1980s but by the middle of the era the pair had a strong rival in Bradford based John Celebanksi. Former amateur international and a popular heavyweight in the town, John had fought British champion John L Gardner on a couple of occasions and once got into trouble over a biting accusation. Landlord of several pubs including *The Royal* in Girlington and the *Lord Clyde* in the city centre, Celebanksi had kept his interest in boxing in the city by taking out a manager's licence and had started to build up a promising stable of boxers from the area. Celebanksi would later add promotion to his talents but in a stable that included Keighley welterweight John Daly, Bradford bantam George Bailey, Nigerian heavyweight Eddie Cooper and the lightweight Rocky Mensah, the ace in the pack at training sessions at Celebanski's base at the transport club gymnasium in Thornton Road was the Manningham, Girlington youngster John Doherty who had started his boxing at the Bradford YMCA club.

In May 1982, John made his pro debut aged nineteen as a bantam on the under card of the Tom Collins versus Trevor Cattouse British lightweight title fight at the Astoria in Leeds. No one in the Astoria that night would realise they were watching a British champion in the making, for after only forty-six seconds the Bradford man's debut was over. Both Doherty and his opponent Taffy Mills of Sunderland came out of their corners exchanging fierce blows. Before John was into any stride a left hook saw him on his seat. Inexperience told as Doherty rose too quickly at a count of only four. His legs were like

John Doherty, Bradford, three times British super featherweight champion 1986, 1989-90 and 1991-92. Photo courtesy of *Telegraph & Argus*.

rubber and before Mills could throw another punch the fight was stopped. John soon brushed the disaster behind him to be unbeaten in his next ten fights.

Four months after the opening defeat he stopped John Lodge in four rounds at Morley and until Pat Cowdell stopped him in his first title defence nearly four years later, the only time John was stopped was when the referee refused to let him carry on after a cut eye against Hull's Stuart Carmichael a boxer whom he had beaten three times in succession in his first nine months as a professional. Now boxing as a featherweight and with only three defeats in his first twenty fights, Celebanksi was keen on his man to take the first step on the way to a title fight. A challenge was made to Hull's Steve Pollard for his Central Area title and John senior arranged for his man to fight Pollard who had not defended it since he had taken the title from Sheffield's Steve Farnsworth the year previously. The action was due to take place in Pollard's backyard at the Tower Theatre but when the Hull boxer pulled out of the fight in an effort to keep Doherty busy the Bradford man appeared as a late substitute on a bill at Stoke replacing unbeaten Keighley lightweight Gary Felvus who had gone down with flu in a bout against local man Clinton Campbell whilst Pat Cowdell was retaining his European super featherweight title the same night in Birmingham, the Stoke promotion ran into problems and there were only two other bouts on the bill. John's fight was switched from six rounds to eight rounds and despite his opponent's half a stone advantage, Campbell could not cope with Doherty's crisp punching.

Never a man with a killer punch he had only three stoppage wins out of twenty-seven by the time he challenged for a British title. John's style was to make full use of the ring and make his opponent chase him. Content to jab from a distance, John's trademark was to move inside quickly when the opportunity arose to score points in quick bursts. Capable of tiring his opponents, Doherty's strengths came in the second half of the fight when he often dropped his more cautious approach to impose himself in the fight.

Promoter Manny Goodall had a smile on his face when a full house was the order in Doherty's next fight. There was a swelling from the Girlington and Whetley Lane pub and club area where John had already accumulated a cult following to see their man fight for his first title. The Central Area fight with Steve Pollard had been switched to The Yorkshire Executive Club in Bradford. There was talk of Pollard struggling to make the weight but John was not taking any chances. Boxing strictly to orders from his corner, Doherty employed his workmanlike job with perfected ease. Pollard did the chasing but it was the Girlington man who did the picking off. Seeing his title slipping away Pollard came strong in the seventh, the only round in which he won. Doherty made sure he won the last round to give Bradford its first Central Area title for five years (Martin Bridge had won the light welter title in 1979).

For his first fight of 1985 Doherty met Mohammed Lovelock in February. John repeated an earlier points victory over the Manchester man. The half a point victory seemed generous to Lovelock who could not confirm his punching reputation despite doing all the stalking. Content to make him miss with a series of smart, defensive moves things started to change in the fifth round when Lovelock nicked John's eye. The cut was the spur, which brought a strong John Doherty finish to clinch the fight with his work in the last three rounds. Michael Marsden of Leeds was chosen as Doherty's opponent in the first Central Area defence and when the pair were matched at Halifax in the champions next outing, Marsden blew his chance by weighing in over the limit. Doncaster journeyman Dean Bramhald who had beaten Marsden in his last fight at Huddersfield and had a legitimate claim had turned up to watch and paid to do so, took Marsden's place at fifteen minutes notice although the fight was non-title. John had beaten Dean on points six months earlier and he repeated the result, a victory which took Doherty's unbeaten run to nine fights and his only defeat in two years had been the cut eye decision against Stuart Carmichael.

Though he moved up the ratings in the featherweight ranks having been in the British top ten since 1984, a title fight with the likes of Barry McGuigan or Pat Cowdell the top two feathers in the country seemed remote, until a situation opened that gave the Bradford man his chance to fight for a British championship. Following on from the World boxing controls in America, the British Boxing Board decided to install two new weight divisions, which were a cruiser (in between light heavyweight and heavyweight) and a junior lightweight/super featherweight range at 9st 4lb. There had been an earlier attempt to establish the latter weight in 1969 but after Jimmy Anderson had won his outright belt the division was withdrawn. Now with double the pro boxers in the game, the board had considered it a fine time to resume the division. Being more comfortable at the new weight Doherty's name was circulated as a possible contender for the new title.

For John's first fight as a super featherweight, promoter Manny Goodall decided to cash in on Doherty's popularity in the city by following up the full house at the Executive Club with a show at the St George's Hall. Not since the 1950s had there been an open hall promotion and John was sharing the top of the bill with Charlie Watson the Bradford welterweight who under Keith Tate's management was unbeaten in his first six fights. The ticket sales went well and Doherty sent the sizable crowd home happy. The taller Dave Pratt who had an inferior record (only twelve wins from twenty-three) was not in the same class. John punched him to a standstill and the crowd witnessed a rare stoppage win by their man. His manager was quick to point out that John's record did not reflect the power of his punching and he was a better puncher than given credit for, a feat he had demonstrated in his six round destruction of Dave Pratt.

John's next fight was his most important yet and one that many consider one of his greatest performances. Clyde Ruan, a twenty-five year old taxi driver from Slough who had been born in St Kitts was rated Britain's number two behind Pat Cowdell and he had fought all the rated featherweights. He had beaten both Pat Doherty and Paul Huggins, two boxers who were in the frame for eliminators in the new division in earlier eliminators for the featherweight title and had lost in his last two fights to World rated Barry McGuigan who knocked him out in four rounds in a British and European challenge and Jim McDonnell who had recently won the newly vacant European title. The fight was an official eliminator, for it was revealed that Pat Cowdell was to fight Pat Doherty for the title in the near future, the winner to fight Manchester based Najib Daho who had beaten Kevin Pritchard in his eliminator and the winner of that to fight the winner of John and Ruan. The calibre of the men on Ruan's record of twenty wins from twenty-five fights which was almost identical to John's nineteen wins and three draws from twenty-five fights made him the strong favourite and though some of John's followers rated his chances, no one could have forecast the landslide victory which he delighted the Bradford crowd with. The Bradford man's confidence was sky high especially after the fight when referee Roland Dakin revealed that John had won every round in his points victory. It was obvious from the middle stages that Ruan needed a knockout to win, though that was never a possibility as Doherty never let up the pressure.

There was speculation that Pat Cowdell who had made an abortive one round attempt at Azamah Nelson's WBC featherweight title would retire after the crushing defeat. In the event the Boxing Board ruled him out and Croyden Irishman Pat Doherty was matched with the Manchester Moroccan Najib Daho for the title. A week before the fight, injury ruled out Daho and though some managers wouldn't have put their man in a big fight on a week's notice, Celebanksi had no hesitation in putting his man in with his namesake on the Preston bill. After some poor recent press Bradford was in the midst of a hit back campaign 'Bradford's Bouncing Back' and the Doherty title bid at Preston story fitted nicely in the champion's niche.

John Doherty proved to be a hero in more ways than one. In a demonstration of skill and raw courage helped by the perfect mental attitude he survived an early points deficit and a cut eye which looked as if it might stop him and which he needed six stitches in afterwards, to become Bradford's first boxing champion. Perhaps overawed by the occasion John made a bad start and allowed Pat to dictate, but by the fifth round he had developed a pattern rhythm, which he kept going to the end of the fight. Referee John Coyle made John the winner by two rounds.

Following on from Doherty's feat of becoming the first Bradford born British champion came the first British title fight in the city when John defended his title against Pat Cowdell. With Daho still out of the picture, the Board could not ignore Cowdell's claim after he had returned to action with a fifth round stoppage win over Steve Griffiths. Manny Goodall and Bernard Land secured the fight for the St George's Hall, with Manny promising the Bradford fighter a European clash in the city if he came through successfully against Cowdell and the awaiting in the wings Najib Daho. Jean Marc Renard who had been beaten by Cowdell in 1984 was European champion again and Goodall was confident Renard who had fought Cowdell in the latter's home town of Birmingham would come to Bradford. Three and a half inches taller and ten years older, Cowdell's record of two World title attempts the first being in Houston where he went fifteen rounds with Salvador Sanchez and five successful European

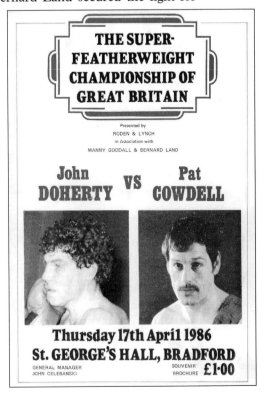

THE SUPER-FEATHERWEIGHT CHAMPIONSHIP OF GREAT BRITAIN

Presented by
RODEN & LYNCH
in Association with
MANNY GOODALL & BERNARD LAND

John DOHERTY VS **Pat COWDELL**

Thursday 17th April 1986
St. GEORGE'S HALL, BRADFORD

GENERAL MANAGER
JOHN CELEBANSKI

SOUVENIR
BROCHURE **£1·00**

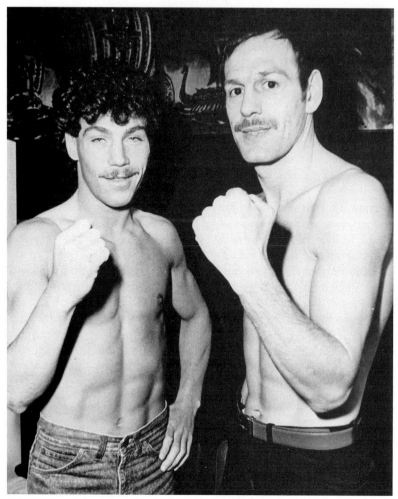

John Doherty and **Pat Cowdell** before their British title fight at St Georges Hall, Bradford, 1986. Photograph courtesy of *Telegraph & Argus*, Bradford.

title fights made him the outstanding favourite, though John did not mind being the underdog which he had been in his last two fights against Ruan and Pat Doherty. Despite commencing his career five years before Doherty (he was British champion and had fought Sanchez before John's first fight). Cowdell had fought only eight more times, though he had won a good percentage of them inside the distance. On the night Cowdell proved he was the master craftsman, whether the occasion got to him was unsure but John boxed too statically and did not move away as much as normal when Cowdell

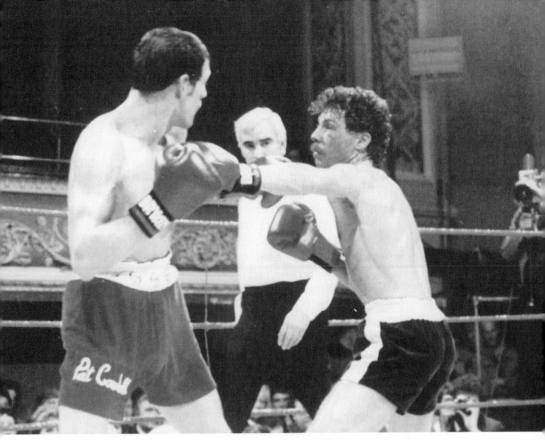

John Doherty tries to line up his right against Pat Cowdell in his unsuccessful defence of the British super featherweight title at the St Georges Hall in 1986. Photograph courtesy *Telegraph & Argus*.

pressurised. As the fight progressed it became too one-sided. Bravery wasn't enough and the referee was forced to stop John for the second time since his first pro defeat.

Surprisingly Cowdell was blasted out in one round by Daho the next month but before Doherty could sustain a challenge to the Moroccan, he would have to earn his spurs again through the eliminators. It was six months before John Doherty was back in the ring. Edging back with sparring sessions with lightweight contender Carl Crooks at Burnley he met his old foe Stuart Carmichael at the Executive Club. Doherty made it four wins out of five against the Hull man with a good work out in a points win. Carmichael surprised him in the first round with a good shot and Doherty had to dig in to get out of trouble, but once the anxious moments were over it was straight forward as Doherty dominated the rest of the fight.

Dave Savage, the Scottish super featherweight champion was

John's first opponent in the eliminator stakes to retain his title. Savage gave Doherty a fight and a fright for John had to dig deep to record a last ditch half a point victory. The fight held at Batley was the Glasgow man's first venture in England and he made John remember it by more ways than one, for the Girlington fighter needed nine stitches and it looked at one time that the referee Sid Nathan would stop it. The opinion was that if the Scot had changed tactics earlier than the midway point when he started to walk through John's defences he might have got the verdict. The stitches meant that John was inactive for three months before meeting Liverpool's Kevin Pritchard in a final eliminator. The shadow of Pat Cowdell loomed over the contest for the former World challenger had been granted a free shot at champion Daho and if Doherty got through Pritchard he would fight the winner. Celebanksi was now into the promotion game and in a joint affair with Leeds promoter Merlin Treymaine, big John booked the old Mecca Dance Hall, now under another new tag 'Dollars Night Scene' (the club had opened in 1960 on the site of the Bradford Roller Skating Rink which had burnt down in 1956. Boxing promotions were held there in the late 1940s and both Bruce Woodcock and Freddie Mills boxed there in exhibition). Over 1,000 attended the nightclub to watch John produce a convincing points win. He won nine of the rounds and had Pritchard down in round seven. Big John, tongue in cheek, had quoted John had looked terrible in training but he looked the part against Pritchard, a man who had been in with both Cowdell and Daho. When Doherty's two rivals met again for the title Cowdell gained revenge and stopped Daho in nine rounds. Celebanksi dispelled doubts on his man meeting Cowdell again. 'He had learnt from the first fight and Daho had shown what could be done in his first fight with Cowdell', big John quoted. Doherty had earned his right for a second tilt at the title by coming through the eliminators whilst Cowdell had got his return with the champion Daho because of who he was.

John's rematch with Cowdell never took place for after the Pritchard fight; the Bradford challenger was out of action for seventeen months with an arthritic back. The unbeaten Welsh featherweight under Frank Warren's management, Floyd Havard, took John's place and beat Cowdell in eight rounds in front of Havard's own crowd in Aberavan. Cowdell never fought again and retired with thirty-six wins from forty-two fights. Doherty had been due to fight American John Boyd on a promotion at Manningham Sports Centre (Del Bryan beat Errol Christie on the same bill) and when he did finally pick up the threads, his warm-up fight for his championship fight was against old opponent Les Walsh. The pair had met three times before. John had won in 1983 and 1984 and there had been a draw in 1984. Walsh was a good choice as Doherty enjoyed a points win workout with the main thing being there was no ring rust.

John's date with Havard took a back seat when John Celebanksi got him his first European title fight. A swelling of Bradford friends and Irish relatives followed Doherty for a St Patrick's Day date in Copenhagen for John's first fight out of England. The Yorkshireman's opponent was a young Dane, Racheed Lawal with a growing reputation as a fearsome puncher. Lawal had beaten a fellow Dane in his last outing to take the title in only his eleventh fight. Despite his limited experience Lawal proved too big a handful for the Girlington fighter. Even John's ring craft and defensive qualities weren't enough. Never comfortable and forced to take the defensive path, a right to the chin from Lawal ended John's European challenge in round four. The other minus from the trip was that a nose injury meant his chance to win back his British super featherweight title from champion Havard had to be put back until September 1989.

Celebanksi forecast an upset when his man travelled to meet the unbeaten champion at Avan Lido. After studying Havard's style, Big John's theory was to take Havard on at close quarters. Always of the opinion John's punching power was far better than acknowledged, Celebanksi worked on sharpening his boxer's hitting for he was well aware that Cowdell did well mixing it for six rounds before running out of steam. Havard was one of the hottest names in the country and match favourite as Doherty upset the odds to re-claim his title. A noticeable fact, jinx if you'd like, was that since the weight division had been resumed, every champion had lost in his first defence. Sticking to his pre-fight plan of harassing Havard, John had no idea his opponent had obtained a hand injury and was as surprised as anyone when he was forced to quit in the eleventh round. Tasting the success of being a British champion again, the win rocketed him to fourth in the WBC ratings. There was talk of another European title fight for Laval had been replaced by Frenchman Daniel Londas and promoter Mickie Duff wanted to put it on at Harrogate. John was adamant he wanted the third title win and an outright Lonsdale Belt for his son Sean and that was his priority.

Manchester boxer Joey Jacobs, who had campaigned as a lightweight and in a short pro career of only twelve fights had beaten the likes of Carl Crook, Neil Haddock and Sugar Gibiluru and lost to Steve Boyle in a British title fight was selected as John's first challenger for his re-won title. Jacob's manager, Jack Trickett, secured the fight for Oldham Sports Centre, the action taking place five months after John had reclaimed his title. The week before the fight, John helped Celebanksi out of a hole when his top of the bill at the Executive Club dropped out with flu and Doherty gave a three round exhibition with Brian Charters. Whilst boxers usually step up in weight rather than down, Big John believed Jacobs camp was seeking an advantage by wanting a 9.00am weigh in, instead of the usual 1.00pm fight weigh in. Was the early reason, which Celebanksi refused to agree an opportunity to strengthen Jacobs up before the action? The rumour had gone round that Jacobs had taken weight off to make the fight and with Jacobs having not gone twelve rounds before, Doherty this time was expected to retain his title. The fight was a very close affair and although Doherty thought he might have nicked it, the former Commonwealth Games medallist Jacobs was the new champion. The fight was a bruising affair with both men bloodied. Doherty gave his all in the quest for the outright belt but he couldn't stave off Jacobs's challenge. Cheered on in a packed hall and in front of his own supporters Jacobs surprisingly came stronger in the latter stages and edged it with his work in the last two rounds. It was a disappointed John Doherty for he had rejected the fight with Daniel Londas to fight Jacobs and now the European title was not available to him.

The month after the Jacobs fight it was reported that Paul Hodgkinson the British featherweight champion had decided to drop his title to concentrate on Europe and World honours. John Morris of the Boxing board had been at the Jacobs fight and it was decided to match John with Sean Murphy the former ABA bantam champion for the vacant title. There was no problem about dropping down to featherweight because Doherty had always felt comfortable about the nine stone mark. Murphy was in Frank Warren's growing stable of champions and as seemed usual John had to travel to his opponent's backyard for his challenge. In Murphy's case it was St Albans. Murphy had won seventeen out of eighteen and was unbeaten in his last ten fights. His only defeat had been a Commonwealth title challenge three years earlier against Ray Mintus. Murphy had never gone past eight rounds and pundits considered Doherty had a more than even chance of becoming a double British champion. As expected it was a fast and furious start with Murphy swarming all over the Bradford man. Matters looked to have changed by round two, for Doherty had cut Murphy's eye and seemed poised to exploit the advantage. By the third round the fight was all over cheered on by his local crowd, Murphy finished Doherty with a left hook, two minutes into the round. John admitted afterwards that the cut eye had made him too complacent. The plan had been to keep away for five or six rounds and he had walked bang into a right. Down for seven he had risen to be finished off by a left hook and a glancing right.

With a retirement after eight years in the ring a possibility the drive that kept Doherty in the sport was the spur of another title fight and the elusive Lonsdale Belt. The jinx of losing the super featherweight title in the first defence in which Doherty had suffered twice continued. Jacobs lost to Franke Ford, who in turn lost to former Doherty victim Kevin Pritchard who had been beaten by Welshman Robert Dickie who had done exceptionally well to come back from a serious car crash, by the time Doherty resumed his ring career. In his 37th fight John came through another eliminator for a crack at his old title. He convincingly beat Newcastle's Frankie Foster on points at the St Andrew's Sporting Club in Glasgow and amazingly the week after Dickie lost his first defence to Toxteth's Sugar Gibiliru. Sugar had been an also ran for the majority of his career. He had fought mostly in the lightweight and light welter ranks and sporting a poor record of only thirteen wins out of fifty he was in the midst of his best ever form as his major upset against Dickie had proved. The twenty-five year old scouser was Doherty's ticket to the belt and he was determined not to blow it again. The Stockport Town Hall action saw a grueling twelve rounds and John was later to give credit to cornermen Keith Tate and Graham Lockwood, who looked after his gashed eye which had happened in the ninth round from a head clash. Sugar did well in the early rounds but had wilted and ran out of steam by the end. Doherty had won his belt and yet again for the eleventh time in succession the champion had lost in his first defence.

John had planned to break the jinx in a return with Gibiliru who ruled himself out of a re-match when he was emphatically beaten by Ilford's Paul Harvey. The six year younger Michael Armstrong from Moston who had unsuccessfully challenged for the Commonwealth featherweight title against African Modest Napuny got the challengers nod, though he had to wait until Doherty's damaged hand had healed. The fight was another Jack Trickett promotion and once again the Doherty fans had to travel to his opponent's home base with the new G.mex in Manchester hosting John's seventh

British title fight in six years. Armstrong started strongly but by the fifth and sixth rounds, Doherty had relaxed into a rhythm and had begun to find the target with a series of good counterpunches. Things looked to be going well, the impression was the longer it went on the more likely that the jinx would be broken. Working to orders to alter Doherty's domination, Armstrong threw a fierce right, which stunned the champion. When he appeared to have got over it a short right poleaxed him at the end of the seventh. The count was interrupted by the bell, but there was no way Doherty could have carried on.

After taking time out Bradford's first outright Lonsdale Belt winner ended his ten year career at the top when he hung up his gloves in 1992. The Jinx on super featherweights ended when Neil Haddock who had defeated Michael Armstrong, the eighteenth fighter to lose his title on his first defence retained the title. As the new century progresses there's a new Doherty on the Bradford boxing scene, for John's son Sean, the driving force to win the outright belt is making rapid strides in the schoolboy and club amateur boxing scene, and in the Girlington ring technician and defensive master young Sean has got a hard act to follow.

CHAPTER 19

Frank Grant

One of British boxing's biggest ever shocks came at Elland Road in 1992 when boxing legend Herol 'Bomber' Graham, whose only four earlier defeats out of forty-eight contests had come at the hands of World champions and had never been beaten by a Briton, lost his British middleweight title to challenging, unheard of outside his hometown Bradford, and Manchester where he trained, scrapper Frank Grant, who remarkably was only in his 23rd professional fight having never boxed as an amateur and only taking up the sport in his early twenties. Even the Boxing Board of Control had thought Grant was on 'mission impossible' for they had failed to bring a new belt to the fight and Frank had to be presented with the one that Graham had won outright.

A West Bowling lad, Frank Grant was living in a bedsit on Canterbury Estate in 1985 when an incident occurred which altered his life's course. A sentence in Walton Jail for assaulting someone he thought had stolen his video gave Grant the opportunity to rethink his life and re-channel his aggression in a more approved direction. For inside he became a fitness freak after promotion to an orderly in the jail's gym, and made a decision to take up serious boxing, a path he was determined to follow on release. Boxing was in the family for Frank's father, Hugh Mackie, had fought professional as a featherweight. Encouraged by his father, Frank began training and sparring down at the Transport Club in Sunbridge Road where the trainer, Maurice Thomas had at one time been trained by Frank's dad. John Celebankski had achieved his first national success as a manager with the rise of John Doherty to the top of the super featherweight ranks and the eager Grant was keen to become an addition to his growing stable of talent.

Though he could laugh about it later, his first paid fight proved a complete disaster and it would be another seven months before he felt comfortable enough to resume after such a traumatic debut. Frankie made his first ring appearance as a twenty-four hour notice substitute at The Yorkshire Executive Club in Bradford and in a

Frank Grant, the Bradford middleweight who produced one of boxing's biggest shock.

hopeless mismatch, he was taken out inside a round by the heavier, light heavyweight Lincoln Pennant. Frank confessed to be 'almost suicidal' after the embarrassment, but his confidence started to come when he made his second appearance in June 1987 and by June the following year, Grant had won six fights in succession of which four had been stopped by the referee. His opponents' experience in the amateur ranks counted for nothing as Brendan Ingle protégé Steve Kofi was stopped in three rounds and Mickie Maw was beaten on points in Gateshead in Maw's pro debut.

By early 1990, Grant's form of thirteen wins out of fifteen saw his name forwarded as an eliminator candidate and he was matched with Kid Milo (real name Winston Walters) at the Midlands Sporting Club in Solihull. The new super middleweight division (twelve stone) had come into being the previous year and the first and current holder was Belfast's Sammy Storey. Originally the eliminator was supposed to be for the middleweight title held by Herol Graham, but when Milo's camp notified the British Boxing Board that their man was unable to make the 11st 6lb limit the board agreed to make the eliminator for the new weight division. Big John, Grant's manager, stated win or lose Frank would still campaign as a middleweight, the fight gave him a double option on the championship front. Milo had in fact lost his unbeaten record in Bradford, when Bradford welterweight Charlie Watson beat him on points in Milo's sixth fight. Frank's fight with the Birmingham boxer went the distance and the Bradford man failed to grasp the opportunity Milo taking the verdict by three rounds (referee John Coyle scored it $98\frac{1}{2}$ to 97).

It was over a year before the Frank Grant boxing career resumed. Following the Milo fight, Frank's mother died and after taking time out after a period of disillusionment when he felt he wanted to return to the ring Frank decided to become a full time boxer and signed for the Manchester manager Tony Martin. Though he laboured heavily Frank made a successful return when he stopped Alan Richards (a late substitute for Tony Booth) in five rounds at Trafford Park. His name shot up the middleweight ratings and his fame in finishing men before the scheduled end of his fights, gave him the local nickname 'the Terminator'. A couple of Americans were beaten, but unfortunately Frank's fame in his hometown attracted an unruly crowd and at a couple of promotions in the city, the police had to quell drink sodden hooligans. Six months after the Richards fight Frank Grant missed his chance to fight the champion Herol Graham. A couple of mishaps in particular the Michael Watson incident (Watson had suffered brain damage and was limited to a wheelchair after his fight with Chris Eubank) had blighted boxing and in an endeavour to portray a cleaner image the Boxing Board of Control had ordered a tighter medical control in the sport. After Frank's brain scan had to be retaken because of a technical fault, the Board's John Morris apologised stating the chance can't be taken but if everything proved all right the fight with Graham, who hadn't fought for a year, would take part later.

Before he met Frank in the title ring a year later in September 1992, Graham had added another notch on his British middleweight title beating John Ashton in six rounds. (Bomber after earlier winning the light middleweight title in 1981 had first won the middleweight title in 1985 and in his second spell as champion he had held the title since 1988), but he had lost his last fight to 'bogey man' Sumbu Kalambay who had now beaten him twice in a European title challenge. The Kalambay defeat had been Graham's fourth defeat in forty-eight contests which had started in 1978. His other two defeats had been in World title fights against the class of Mike McCallum and Julian Jackson. Three weeks before the fight, Phil Martin was predicting the 'time was right for Grant'. Admittedly Graham was not the fighter he was, the question was after fourteen years in the business did he still possess the ambition and drive to get back on to the World's stage. The fight was on an Elland Road extravaganza which had Yorkshire's own KO King Henry Wharton fighting Fidel Castro as the top of the bill. Henry was defending his Commonwealth super middleweight title and challenging holder Fidel Castro who was going for his outright Lonsdale Belt for the British super middleweight title. Wharton was big news in Leeds and because he had sold out Leeds Town Hall a few times, his manager Mickie Duff had no hesitation in booking the bigger Leeds United football ground. Though Wharton was the big headliner, Bradford's Frank Grant was the man who dominated the newspaper headlines the next day. Martin's plan was to make it as difficult as possible by staying with Graham. After the fight he admitted his biggest problem was to get Frank's mind in the right tune with his strengths. Only his pals at the Champs Training Centre in the rough area of Moston and his growing army of Bradford fans gave him a chance as the fight went exactly to plan. Mickie Duff described the fateful ninth round where Grant became champion in his twenty-third fight, as one of the best rounds he had ever seen in his life. Graham started to pick up the pace in the seventh round. He was probably just ahead on points and for the first time he looked to hurt Grant. In the eighth Graham decided to go for victory as he built on a solid left with three more quick punches. The champion could not stop the strong willed Grant from counter punching and the challenger finished the round the stronger. After thirty seconds into round nine Grant trapped his opponent on the ropes and Graham did well to hang on as a rapid fire of left and right hooks had him floundering. As Graham came away Grant refused to lay off and stalked him with more big left hands one of which sprawled him to the canvas. He was up at the count of nine as Grant, urged on by his followers, went in for the kill and he didn't let them down as the referee was forced to stop it before the round ended. Bradford and Britain had a new champion and Wharton made it a Yorkshire double by taking the super middleweight title off Castro.

Whilst efforts were being made to find the last British champion who had not boxed as an amateur, Eric Boon during the War was quoted but as he had been a pro at sixteen it was an unfair comparison, Martin insisted his man still had a lot to learn but could go further in the game. Graham admitted to weight problems and though he felt fit he stated afterwards he had been surprised how he had tired quickly. Experts predicted an end to Graham's career. He did retire but after Grant's career had finished, Graham made another comeback and fought for another World title in his late thirties.

Mickie Duff talked of 'doing a Wharton' with Frank and putting on a European title fight at Valley Parade after being impressed with the turn out for Grant's first defence at St George's Hall. Frank's fight with challenger, Alfreton's John Ashton who had made unsuccessful challenges for the European (Sumbu Kalambay), Commonwealth (Richie Woodall) and British titles (Graham) was the second title fight at the hall, following on from the John Doherty versus Pat Cowdell clash of 1986. Before the action started Ashton's

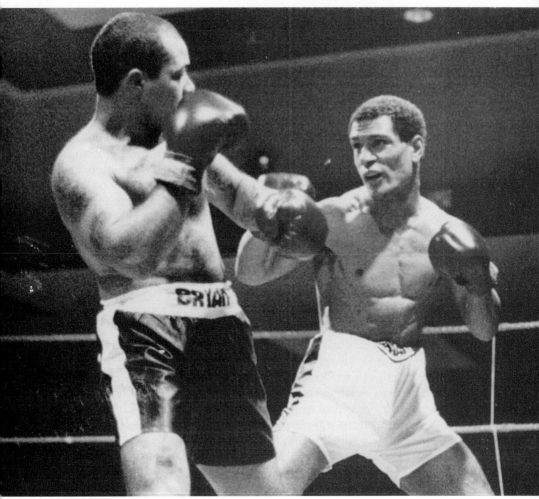

Frank Grant, Bradford, left attacks in one of the early fights at the Sporting Club, Bradford. *Photograph courtesy of Telegraph & Argus.*

manager protested about the ring being too small and after it was re-assembled he still was not happy and an agreement was made that if the ring size played any part in his boxer's defeat, the Boxing Board would sanction a re-match. Once again the tournament hit trouble and the police had to be brought in to quell over-zealous spectators who wanted to imitate the men in the ring. It was Ashton who copped all the trouble. The Midlands man compared it to 'like being hit by a truck' as Grant's relentless powered pressure forced Ashton's corner to surrender their man's challenge from the in-between-round stool. Though Frank's performance didn't satisfy the purists, power and strength made up for his lack of ring craft. The same critics, perhaps forgetting that Frank, without any amateur experience and only twenty-five fights under his belt was still learning his trade. His win saw his World ratings jump to eighth in the WBC (champion Gerald McLellan) and sixth in the IBF (Champion Roy Jones).

The trouble in his Bradford fights at both the St George's Hall and the Maestro's nightclub saw Martin reluctantly switch Frank's Lonsdale Belt quest to Grant's second home in Manchester. The champion's opponent was Neville Brown who under Mickie Duff's management had won twenty-one out of twenty-two fights. His only set back had been against Paul Wesley, a defeat he had later avenged. Brown had the luxury of the guidance of Brendan Ingle and as usual the wily Irishman had done his homework. He had been there when Grant had beaten Graham and he had worked out Frank's shortcomings. Grant came forward from the first bell trying to work and pressurise Brown who found his distance with a series of solid lefts into Grant's face. This pattern lasted four rounds with the occasional shot shaking Grant. Brown couldn't stop the relentless stalking and there was the glimmer of doubt that Grant had taken all he could throw. It was suspected Grant's fitness would take over in the later stages until Frank obtained a cut in round six. Frank's lack of experience was exposed as he turned to desperation. Brown saw his moment and took complete advantage with the result that the referee stopped the fight in round seven and lifted Brown's hand as Britain's new middleweight champion. Brown made five successful defences until Glenn Catley beat him in 1998. He lost to Steve Collins in a WBO super middleweight challenge in 1996 and was still fighting for titles in 2000.

After time to rethink Frank decided to drop out of boxing. In a Telegraph & Argus interview he confessed he had come to hate boxing: 'If I'd realised what it's all about I'd never have fought' he exclaimed though he quickly added that boxing had given him the chance to change his life and be somebody. 'Money was the motivation and boxing was a means to an end' the ex-champion stated. Like many ex-fighters Frank had a spell in the licensed trade taking a couple of pubs in the city and was later reported working as a driver in Bradford. As the city rejoices with a new champion in Bobby Vanzie, no one can take away Frank Grant's once piece of ring history, which saw him go all the way to a British title and put his name on record as the only Briton to beat a man who is regarded as possibly the greatest boxer never to win a World title.

CHAPTER 20

Peter Judson

espite an array of talent in the thirties and several promising
fighters like Gary Felvus in later years, Keighley had to wait
until May 1998 for its first British title challenger when
Peter Judson got the reward of nine years ring service which had
included taking many fights as a late substitute and on occasions
starving himself to make a short notice weight. Several of his losses
were controversial, but despite the often lack of preparation Peter
was nicknamed 'Bulldog' a tribute to his spirit and ability which he
never lost faith in.

Peter started as a nine year old in Paddy Quinlan's gym but
decided boxing was not for him, a decision he changed five years
later, four years on again he had joined the pro ranks.

Making his debut aged nineteen, Judson commenced his paid
career in Bradford with a six round draw against Darryl Petit in
Bradford. Before he was twenty-one Pete had clocked up seventeen
fights winning nine and losing seven. His eighteenth fight was his
first chance at a title, the occasion went the twelve round distance (in
ten years in the game no one ever stopped him) but Judson couldn't
prevent Russell Davidson repeat an earlier points win in a clash for
the vacant central area featherweight title.

Following the second Davidson defeat, Peter's form began to
become more consistent and after a couple of setbacks he remained
unbeaten from 1992 to 1995. Judson was under Frank Warren's
umbrella and it was one of boxing's big names who finally broke the
run. Colin McMillan had won an outright Lonsdale Belt and had
held the WBO title until Steve Robinson had taken it off him in
1993. McMillan on the comeback trail beat the Keighley man over
eight rounds. Two more defeats followed against Daniel Alicca and
Cassius Baloyi; Warren's influence helped Judson progress from a
club fighter to fighting on championship promotions. Pete was due
to fight on the Nigel Benn versus Steve Collins WBO super
middleweight clash at the Nymex arena in Manchester for his first
international title. Judson was matched with Welshman Dean Phillips

for the vacant IBF inter-continental super featherweight title. The Keighley boxer was shattered with the news prior to his entry into the ring that the medics were unhappy about his brain scan. It looked like his career was over and as he contemplated a life outside the ring, Judson was relieved to get the all clear a couple of months later to fight Phillips.

The fight was Peter's thirty-fifth of which he had lost seventeen. Though all his defeats had gone the distance, Judson didn't have a punching reputation only stopping two men in his eight years in the game.

Building for a distance fight as usual, Judson's plan was to wear Phillips down. The plan succeeded and when the action reached ten gruelling rounds Phillip's challenge was over. Judson was able to produce the finishing blows as he sent the exhausted Welshman to the canvas. There was a big worry when Phillips collapsed afterwards but thankfully it was only exhaustion.

Six months later he was matched against stablemate Barry Jones another Welshman. Jones was unbeaten in sixteen fights over four years and considered World title material. Judson lost his title at Hillsborough Leisure Centre. It was another year before Peter Judson fought again. Charlie Shepherd born in Burnley and boxing out of Carlisle had originally campaigned as a lightweight and had made an unsuccessful challenge against British champion Michael Ayres in that division. Moving down to super featherweight Shepherd had lost his first tilt at the title against PJ Gallagher but had since won the title and his fight against Judson was his second defence. Fighting for his outright belt Shepherd met a Yorkshireman stacked with resilience and bravery. Peter made a bright start before he faded. The seventh was his best round when it looked like the tide might turn. Judson stunned the champion but could not follow it up and Shepherd finished the stronger to keep his title.

In his thirties the Judson career looked to be over, but he was down on the Mike Tyson bill at Hampden though because the promotion overran he never appeared.